ALL-AMERICAN SPIRIT

© 2021 RDA Enthusiast Brands, LLC.
1610 N. 2nd St., Suite 102
Milwaukee, WI 53212-3906

International Standard Book Number: 978-1-62145-745-9

Library of Congress Control Number: 2021933639

Component Number: 117300106H

FRONT COVER COLORIZATION
Sanna Dullaway

PHOTO CREDITS

Front cover Afro Newspaper/Gado/Getty Images; **4** AP/Shutterstock; **6** Bettmann Archive/Getty Images; **7** *t* Orlando/ Three Lions/Getty Images; **7** *b* Bettmann Archive/Getty Images; **8** *l* Courtesy of Library of Congress, LC-DIG-ds-04926; **10** *t* Bettmann Archive/Getty Images; **10** *b* Andrew D. Bernstein/Getty Images; **11** Courtesy of Library of Congress, LC-DIG-ppmsca-18459; **22** *t* JDC/AP/Shutterstock; **23** Dean Conger/Corbis/Getty Images; **30** Photoshot/Getty Images; **31** *t* United Archives/Getty Images; **31** *bl* Express/Getty Images; **31** *br* Michael Ochs Archives/Getty Images; **32** Deborah Mueske; **36** *t* Courtesy National Park Service, photo by Michael Quinn; **36** *b* Courtesy National Park Service; **37** *t* Courtesy National Park Service; **37** *dam* Tupungato/Shutterstock; **37** *bird* David Calhoun/Shutterstock; **37** *rafting* Courtesy National Park Service, photo by Michael Quinn; **39** *map* Christina Spalatin; **40** Gimas/Shutterstock; **41** Steve Lagreca/ Shutterstock; **42** Library of Congress, Prints and Photographs Division, HAER WYO,15-YELNAP,3--11 (CT); **43** *t* Iconographic Archive/Alamy Stock Photo; **43** *b* f8 archive/Alamy Stock Photo; **45** *Yosemite* Sharon Gilbert; **45** *br* ivan-96/Getty Images; **48** *b* Courtesy Mary Nowacek; **49** Anonymous/AP/Shutterstock; **52** Bettmann Archive/Getty Images; **53** *t* George Rose/Getty Images; **53** *b* Archive Photos/Getty Images; **54-57** *color images* Jeff Riggins, Hoosier Property Media, Courtesy of Kelly Huff; **55** *black and white images* Courtesy of the Ohio History Connection; **58** Bettmann Archive/Getty Images; **59** *paint* YvanDube/Getty Images; **59** *polaroid* Science & Society Picture Library/Getty Images; **60** vintageamericanpottery.com; **61** Str/AP/Shutterstock; **64** Bettmann Archive/Getty Images; **65** *tl* David H. Wells/Getty Images; **65** *tr* Bettmann Archive/Getty Images; **65** *b* Courtesy of Science History Institute; **66** Spencer Weiner/Getty Images; **67** *t* Library of Congress, LC-DIG-fsa-8a03407; **67** *b* Courtesy of Library of Congress, LC-DIG-npcc-00292; **68** *t* Library of Congress, LC-USF34-024865-D; **68** *b* Boston Globe/Getty Images; **69** Bob Wands/Shutterstock; **70-71** © Zamboni Co. Archives; **72** Nara Archives/Shutterstock; **73** *calculator* DeGolyer Library, Southern Methodist University; **73** *team and Grace* Grace Murray Hopper Collection, Archives Center, National Museum of American History, Smithsonian; **74** University of Southern California/Getty Images; **75** *t* Natalya Danko/Getty Images; **75** *b* Bettmann Archive/Getty Images; **78** FCA; **79, 84** Bettmann Archive/Getty Images; **85** *t* Minnesota Historical Society/Corbis/Getty Images; **85** *b* PhotoQuest/Getty Images; **86-87** Campbell Soup Co.; **90** *t* Courtesy Burger King; **90** *bl* Starbucks Coffee Co.; **90** *br* PhotoQuest/Getty Images; **92** Courtesy Library of Congress, #LOC-LC-DIG-highsm-12949; **93** Courtesy of McDonald's; **94** Everett Collection/Shutterstock; **95** *bl* Everett Collection/Shutterstock; **98** *l* Underwood Archives/Getty Images; **98** *r* Michael Neelon(misc)/Alamy Stock Photo; **99** *tr* Bobby Bank/Getty Images; **99** *bl* Courtesy State Library of North Carolina Digital Collections, #13694212; **99** *br* Wonder Bread; **100** *tr* Franck Fotos/Alamy Stock Photo; **102** Bettmann Archive/Getty Images; **103** *t* US Army/Interim Archives/Getty Images; **103** *bl, br* Bettmann Archive/Getty Images; **110** *bl* Chris Pfuhl/AP/Shutterstock; **112** Courtesy of Library of Congress, LC-DIG-fsac-1a35314; **114** Harris & Ewing—Washington, D.C.; **119** Courtesy of K.B. Getz; **120** FPG/Getty Images; **125** Galerie Bilderwelt/Getty Images; **128** Bettmann Archive/Getty Images; **129** AP/Shutterstock; **130** National Archives and Records Administration; **131** Bettmann Archive/Getty Images; **134** Ernst Haas/Hulton Archive/Getty Images; **135** Bettmann Archive/Getty Images; **144** Courtesy of Library of Congress, LC-DIG-cwpb-04348; **146** *l* Ernst Haas/Getty Images; **147** Three Lions/Getty Images; **148** The U.S. National Archives and Records Administration; **150, 151, 153** Bettmann Archive/Getty Images; **154** FPG/Hulton Archive/ Getty Images; **155** *t* E. F. Joseph/Anthony Potter Collection/Getty Images; **155** *bl* FPG/Getty Images; **155** *br* Killian/Library of Congress/Corbis/VCG via Getty Images; **156, 158** Peace Corps; **169** Stan Tess/Alamy Stock Photo; **174** Central Press/ Getty Images; **175** *t* National Archive/Getty Images; **175** *b* John Rodgers/Getty Images; **176** Bettmann Archive/Getty Images; **180** Courtesy Ronald Reagan Presidential Library; **183** John F. Kennedy Presidential Library and Museum, Boston; **184** *FDR* Courtesy of Library of Congress, LC-DIG-hec-47235; **184** *poster* Donald Wilson, John F. Kennedy Presidential Library and Museum; **184** *supporters* Sven Walnum, The Sven Walnum Photograph Collection. John F. Kennedy Presidential Library and Museum, Boston; **185** University of Kentucky Digital Library; **187** Walt Zeboski/AP/ Shutterstock; **188-189** NASA; **190** *three images on left* NASA/Johnson Space Center; **192** Bettmann Archive/Getty Images; **193** Michael Ochs Archives/Getty Images; **194** *t* Courtesy of Library of Congress, LC-USW3-033841-C; **194** *b* Courtesy of Library of Congress, LC-USZ62-79898; **195** *l* Courtesy of Library of Congress, LC-USW33-054944-ZC; **195** *r* The New York Public Library, b15591219; **196** *t* William Gottlieb/Getty Images; **196** *b* Everett Collection/Shutterstock; **197** LOC, Carl Van Vechten Collection, LC-USZ62-94955; **198** Warner Bros. Pictures/Getty Images; **199** Warner Bros/Shutterstock; **200** Silver Screen Collection/Getty Images; **202** Gene Lester/Getty Images; **203** Everett Collection Inc/Alamy Stock Photo; **204-205** Gilles Petard/Getty Images; **206-207** Michael Ochs Archives/Getty Images; **photo frames** Eileen Mattison and Betty Remsh

CONTENTS

After Congress approved the Alaska statehood bill in June 1958, Romer Derr, 23, rang a replica of the Liberty Bell 49 times outside the Federal Building in Juneau, AK. Joining him, from left, were Judy Findlay and Marilee Nowacki. President Eisenhower signed the official proclamation on Jan. 3, 1959. ★

CELEBRATING OUR COUNTRY

Remember the special bonds we share as citizens of the great USA in this patriotic collection of stories and photographs from readers of *Reminisce* magazine.

Memories of Little League, family vacations to favorite national parks, and innovations such as the first microwave will bring a smile to your face. Included here are a slew of American-made products. Take a look at the giant Harvard Mark I computation machine, the ancestor of the calculator. And don't forget fast and fun cars! Plus, dig in to some history on America's favorite foods.

We pay homage to the men and women who served our country and those who helped at home; to determined immigrants; to steadfast advocates for civil rights; and to the work ethic of teachers, first responders, farmers and many more.

Finally, we close with a look back at those who had a great impact on us, from Oval Office occupants to the Apollo 11 astronauts and popular stars.

Like Romer Derr, pictured at left, we are proud to declare our inclusion in this nation.

THE EDITORS OF *REMINISCE* MAGAZINE

STAR-SPANGLED PASTIMES

Whether it's a round of pickup baseball or the school's winning shot at homecoming, Americans love a good game and bonding over the excitement.

Paul Arms, far left, looks over his heroes' stats on his Topps cards; University of Maryland football cheerleaders raise a shout for their team; and the Chicago Bears' Gale Sayers (40) finds an open spot over teammate Bob Wallace (89), rushing for 20 yards against the Cleveland Browns in 1969.

John adored the Washington Senators through the 1950s, despite their lousy record. ★

HOPE IS ONLY A SEASON AWAY

EVEN A LOSING TEAM CAN WIN A KID'S HEART.

L et's understand this from the start: I like football, basketball, soccer, golf and a lot of other sports. But baseball is special.

I grew up in the Virginia suburbs of Washington, D.C., in the 1950s. The Washington Senators were my guys. I'm sure everyone has heard the old saw: Washington—first in war, first in peace and last in the American League. No matter, that was the team I loved.

As a kid, I collected baseball cards, as did most of my friends. We prized Senators over Yankees every time. Trading my Yogi Berra for a Yo-Yo Davalillo might not make sense to a lot of people. After all, Yo-Yo played only 19 Major League games. But they were all with the Senators. I remember watching him in a pregame warmup throw a baseball from the shortstop position clear over the left field wall of old Griffith Stadium. No mere mortal could throw that far.

Heated discussions in my circle of friends involved such issues as who was the best center fielder. Mickey Mantle? Willie Mays? There even were some who pushed for Jimmy Piersall. Sorry, it was Jim Busby of the Senators. Case closed. There

was not a better hitter in the league than Mickey Vernon, our first baseman. And who can forget Pete Runnels at shortstop, or Wayne Terwilliger at second base? Pitching? Bob Porterfield, Camilo Pascual and Pedro Ramos all the way.

Why, oh why, with all this talent, could we not finish above last place? Truth be told, the Senators did finish next to last a couple of times. Thank goodness for the Kansas City A's. Things were looking good in 1960, when my boys made it to fifth place. Then disaster struck.

Club owner Calvin Griffith moved the team to Minneapolis, Minnesota, where they became the Twins. I wrote to *Sport* magazine bemoaning the loss. The editors published my letter, but it didn't bring back my guys.

I never got attached to later iterations of Washington baseball. I moved away from the area after college and now live outside Atlanta. I've adopted the Braves, but they'll never hold the same spot in my heart as my beloved Senators.

On the other hand, I still hate the Yankees.

JOHN A. BROADWELL SENECA, SC

BASEBALL BOYS OF SUMMER

IMAGINATION AND DETERMINATION WERE ALL THEY NEEDED TO PLAY THE GAME THEY LOVED SO MUCH.

S houts of joy erupted as my buddies and I ran out of Caledonia Grade School in Cleveland Heights, Ohio, in June 1941. It was the end of school, the beginning of summer recess. Now we could play our favorite game—baseball—all summer, every day.

Our baseball heroes at the time were Lou Boudreau, Bob Feller and their Cleveland Indians teammates. As young boys, intoxicating thoughts of being discovered by a big-league scout and reaching "the show" filled our daydreams. Never mind the odds against such a thing.

We rarely had enough players to make a team. So we got creative and devised a unique version of the game, something we called two-up rotation. There were usually five or six players: a pitcher, two batters and a few outfielders. If we were short on outfielders, we drew an imaginary line from the large tree looming in center field through second base. Hit the ball past that line and you were out. When an out was called, everyone would rotate to the next position. We never kept score.

We played every day until daylight abandoned us, never breaking for lunch and always reluctant to stop for dinner. Our mothers knew exactly where to find us: at the vacant lot on the corner of Greyton and Taylor roads, in a field whose most noticeable feature was the distinct outline of a diamond worn through the grass by the baseball boys of summer.

For many years after my early youth, I continued to play ball: in high school,

Tommy Smith (above left, with Gene Pfeiffer) came up with his own version of baseball in the summer of 1941.

college and an amateur league. I was even offered pro contracts by the Indians and the Philadelphia Phillies but chose to stay in college instead.

Nothing was quite as special and pure as those two-up rotation games. It's a treasured memory from when the life of a 10-year-old boy was as perfect as it could be.

THOMAS P. SMITH CHARDON, OH

WITH A WINK AND A NOD

ON A TRIP WITH MY DAD to Shibe Park in Philadelphia to watch my beloved Athletics in the summer of 1949, my real purpose in going was to see Ted Williams play for the first time.

I followed Ted in the box scores every day. It seemed to me, at 7 years old, that Ted always had two or three hits every time I looked. After checking Ted's statistics, I always peeked at my team, the Athletics. Most of the time, they registered another defeat.

As we settled into our seats behind the Boston Red Sox dugout to watch batting practice, my heart raced while I looked in all directions for number 9, Ted Williams. There he was in the outfield, playing catch with his buddy Johnny Pesky.

Soon he started walking toward the infield for batting practice and went to the plate to hit. *Crack! Crack! Bang! Bang!* The balls hit the right-field wall. His line drives sounded like a cannon shot.

Then my dad, always a leather lung, prodded me to stand up as Ted walked toward us in our seats about

Ted Williams certainly had a presence on the field, and to a 7-year-old boy he meant the world. ★

eight rows behind the dugout. "Hey, Ted!" yelled my dad, loud enough for the whole park to hear. Ted looked up quickly, right at me, and winked.

I was on cloud nine. I had never been more thankful for my dad's booming voice. Wow! Ted Williams winked at me.

WILLIAM BARNA SLATINGTON, PA

BETTER LATE THAN NEVER

In the mid-1980s, my brother, his wife, my husband and I went to a game at Dodger Stadium in Los Angeles. The Dodgers were playing the San Francisco Giants that day, and the Giants were on fire.

By the middle of the ninth inning, the Giants were comfortably ahead and at least a third of the capacity crowd had packed up and left in disappointment. All of a sudden, in the bottom of the ninth, the Dodgers woke up and scored a ton of runs to win the game.

The remaining fans went berserk! We screamed ourselves hoarse during that half inning. I couldn't speak clearly for two whole days. That was the most exciting baseball game I have ever seen.

JAN CROSS HENDERSON, NV

Awaiting a turn at the plate, Babe Ruth, left, and Ernie Shore of the American League's Boston Red Sox, 1916, stay alert. ★

MAKING FRIENDS WITH THE BABE

MY GRANDUNCLE Arthur Augustus "Ben" Egan helped put Sherrill, New York, on the map for its contribution to baseball history. Ben and his nine brothers constituted the local semipro baseball team, and Uncle Ben went on to play professional ball with the Philadelphia Athletics, Boston Red Sox and Cleveland Indians.

During his career as a pro ball player, Ben played alongside George Herman "Babe" Ruth and became a friend of his. Ben is credited with being the Babe's first professional catcher. Both played for the International League's Baltimore Orioles in 1914. In July of that year, both were traded to the Boston Red Sox for cash, along with pitcher Ernie Shore.

SHIRLEY LENNON De BELLA ROME, NY

BASEBALL ICON

George Herman "Babe" Ruth, aka the Great Bambino and the Sultan of Swat, spent 12 years at St. Mary's Industrial School for Boys, a Catholic reformatory school in Baltimore, Maryland, before signing with the Baltimore Orioles in 1914 at age 19.

Before the end of the 1914 season, Ruth was traded to the Boston Red Sox, where, due to a crowded roster, he spent time pitching for the Red Sox's minor league team, the Providence Grays.

Ruth's pitching took the Grays to the International League pennant that year and got him a permanent position in the Red Sox rotation the following year.

As a pitcher for Boston, Ruth accrued impressive numbers. But it was his swing that drove the rest of his career. In December 1919, he was sold to the New York Yankees, a deal that haunted Boston fans and was known as "the curse of the Bambino."

At New York, Ruth and company won seven pennants and four World Series titles. When he retired in 1935 from the Boston Braves, he held 56 major league records, including the most home runs hit—714—a record that lasted 39 years.

Some Campbell Sash team members take a group shot with other Little Leaguers. ★

FROM BATBOY TO ALL-STAR

SKILLS FOR THE GAME AND MEMORIES FOR A LIFETIME.

After spending two years as a batboy for the Campbell Sash Little League team in my hometown of Campbell, Ohio, I was ready to play ball. I arrived at the spring tryouts in 1954 with my birth certificate stating my age—Little League baseball back then was for boys 9 through 12—and a lot of excitement. I signed the registration form in return for a large numbered tag that I pinned to the back of my shirt and wore throughout the tryouts.

Each manager and coach carried a clipboard to rate the players they wanted on their teams. On the last day of tryouts, we left and waited for a call. Happily, I got one from the manager of the same team where I had served as a batboy.

The next day we got our uniforms and black shoes with rubber cleats. I was thrilled to play on our field.

It felt just like a miniature Major League field—with green grass, a soft dirt-and-sand infield and honest-to-goodness dugouts.

The year I turned 12 was especially memorable for me. In previous years, I had been a regular season starter and made the all-star team. But that year I won the batting title with a .550 average, and as a pitcher, I went 5 and 1. Our all-star team won the Ohio State Little League championship, beating Bridgeport 9-4. The opposing pitcher, Joe Niekro, went on to be a Major League pitcher—and I hit a line drive off of him.

Our town celebrated with a parade down Main Street. Standing on the city fire truck, we were proud to be champs for a day.

KENNETH G. ZBELL MICHIGAN CITY, IN

DO GET FRESH WITH ME

Whether at a game, at the movies or at home,
a burst of chewy mint is a nice refreshing break.

Packed with Glamour

Big makers like Wrigley and Beech-Nut saw their dominance of the "nickel gum" trade fall with shortages of sugar and other ingredients during WWII. After the war, smaller "penny gum" makers moved in on the $90 million market. Here, Bowman Gum links its Warrens Mint Cocktail with Hollywood's dazzling lifestyle.

Quick Pick-Me-Up

Bubble gum had been popular with kids since about 1930, but mint gum was seen as an adult product. So a Wrigley's Spearmint ad featuring children was unusual—but this one ran in *Family Circle* and its chief target is the busy mom eager for a "fine little lift."

PICTURES FROM THE PAST
★ ★ ★ Play Ball! ★ ★ ★

MOTLEY CREW

This photo includes my daddy, standing in the bottom row, far left, and his baseball buddies in 1913. Baseball was good clean fun 100-plus years ago. Motley or not, these boys grew up to be fine men.

JEAN L. McCOY McMAHON
MOUNTVILLE, PA

UNEXPECTED HERO ⩗

The summer of 1965, Dad signed me up for baseball. My lack of skills got me on a team nicknamed "The Losers." But during the last game of the season, we were up by one run in the bottom of the ninth. Then a ball was hit to me in center field. I charged forward, lost the ball in the sun, but continued running until—miracle of miracles—I felt the ball land in my mitt. It was the last out of the game, our first and only win, and I was the team hero. I have to admit, winning felt so good.

LARRY SCHROEDER KEMP, TX

WELCOME ESCAPE ⩓

Baseball occupied my thoughts while the war raged overseas. I was a center fielder on the team from St. Adalbert's.

FRANK KUCA O'FALLON, IL

FULL OF SMILES

I found this photo taken in 1951 of my cousin JoAnn (standing next to the woman in street clothes) and JoAnn's softball team in Woodstock, Illinois. Each player had to provide her own shoes, and each girl looks happy and strong.

CONNIE CANTRELL LITTLETON, CO

CLINCHING A VICTORY

During the summer of 1964, I played for the Pony League All-Stars in Lancaster, California. It was the semifinal game of the District A playoff, and the score was tied 2–2 in extra innings. With a man on base, I hit a fastball over the center-field fence for a home run. My team won 4–2, and they stayed alive to play another game.

ALLAN SCHARTON COPPELL, TX

EVERYTHING'S COMING UP ROSE BOWL

The 1958 Rose Bowl game pitted the Ducks of the University of Oregon against the Ohio State University Buckeyes. California sportswriters were calling it the "worst mismatch of the ages," and oddsmakers had the "ugly ducklings" a 19-point underdog.

But the sportswriters were wrong. Final score: Ohio State 10, Oregon 7. Oregon fans were so jubilant that you'd have thought the Ducks had won.

I was secretary to the Oregon football coaching staff and was so proud of my bosses and the team members. They were winners in my playbook!

REBECCA TOWLER FALKNER EL PASO, TX

★ The Oregon Ducks, foreground, warm up before the Rose Bowl game against Ohio State on New Year's Day 1958.

Ida Dlabal of Wilson, KS, passed along these historical family shots of a Tournament of Roses parade. ★

MUDDY GOOD FUN

While at the University of Southern California, I went to my first Rose Bowl parade and game in 1955—and it was one of the few times in Rose Bowl history that it rained. We enjoyed every wet and cold minute, though we lost to Ohio State.

The biggest excitement came after the game. Much of the fan parking was on an adjacent golf course, where the vehicles didn't play well with the sopping wet grass and dirt. My buddy Larry had a 1948 four-wheel-drive Dodge pickup. We sloshed around for hours pulling fancy cars out of the mud with that ugly truck.

GENE McMEANS HIGHLAND, CA

=== ★★★ ===

A LEGEND IN ACTION

The first bowl game I remember going to was the 1964 Cotton Bowl, in which the University of Texas played Navy, with Heisman Trophy winner Roger Staubach as Navy's quarterback. Texas won 28-6. No one knew at the time that Staubach would later return to the Cotton Bowl as quarterback for the Dallas Cowboys. The Cowboys played their home games in the Cotton Bowl through the 1960s.

JOHN WILKINSON CORPUS CHRISTI, TX

WHIRLWIND TOUR

IN MY SOPHOMORE YEAR at Ohio State, the Buckeyes beat the University of Michigan 12-10 to get to the Rose Bowl.

After Christmas, five buddies and I took a school-chartered flight to California and stayed with friends in Long Beach. We spent four days sightseeing at Disneyland; Las Vegas; Tijuana, Mexico; and Beverly Hills. On New Year's Eve, we headed to the Ambassador Hotel on Wilshire Boulevard in Los Angeles, where the rest of the group was staying.

We toasted the New Year twice, once at 9 p.m. in honor of Ohio time and again at midnight to honor local time. After downing several aspirin at 5:30 the next morning—New Year's Day 1975—we boarded a bus for the parade.

Then on to the Rose Bowl—what a sight! I was sitting at the base of the San Gabriel Mountains, and it was sunny and 71 degrees. And the game between OSU and the University of Southern California was exciting until the final minutes, when Ohio State lost 18-17 on a 2-point conversion by USC.

BILL NEUMAN PITTSBURGH, PA

Scenes from the Rose Bowl game and morning parade on New Year's Day 1975. ★

CHARITY CHEERLEADERS

SPECIAL FOOTBALL SEASON WILL NEVER FADE FROM MEMORY.

Football was the single hottest sport in Massachusetts in the '50s. In the autumn of 1957, when I was a senior and a cheerleader, our high school football team won the Class A state championship. As football players and cheerleaders, we were the kings and queens of the school. For residents of the city, it was like winning the lottery and going to Disney World all in the same day.

Although Disney World didn't yet exist, everyone involved—players, majorettes, band members and, of course, cheerleaders—was invited to Florida to play Miami Edison High in the Orange Bowl. Our only problem was money. We didn't have any. Flying was still a big deal in the '50s, not commonplace like today; we needed to get enough cash to buy 100 round-trip tickets to Florida, a hefty sum.

Our solution was to conduct a door-to-door begging campaign. Lawrence was never a rich city, but residents responded generously to our fundraising, and we all took off to play the December game. We were amazed at how easily we had raised thousands of dollars in three weeks.

We flew down in a small prop plane through a lot of turbulence; most of us had never flown before and were scared to death. In the end, we lost the game in Miami by 40 points. The temperature was a cold 40 degrees for five days, which was not ideal. But that didn't matter to us: We had played and cheered in the Orange Bowl! The

Nothing could stop these cheerleaders and their team from playing at the Orange Bowl in 1957, or swimming in the hotel pool!

weather didn't even stop us from swimming in the ice-cold hotel pool. I know that we'll always remember that football season.

TAMMY FINN YORK, ME

HOMECOMING GAME WAS EVERYTHING

A WIN MEANT MORE TO THE PLAYERS THAN THE COACH KNEW.

I t was 1962, and I was the new football coach of Cambridge High School in Ohio. Our record was 2–3 when mighty Marietta, an Ohio River team, came to our place to play for homecoming. We were an independent school that took what games we could. Marietta was undefeated and ranked eighth among the large division schools.

The week before the big game, I was watching Louisiana State in action on TV. LSU ran a trick play and scored. I shot off the couch and drew up the play on a piece of paper. This play, I determined, would be the key to our victory.

I recalled how then-coach Ray Elliot of Illinois would always pick the toughest team on his schedule for homecoming. He would tell his players, "No one beats Illinois on our homecoming." I was going to sell the same philosophy to our team.

Monday came, and before practice, I held a meeting and had every player take a permanent marker and write on each forearm "Beat Marietta." Out on the field, I showed them the play and told them this was how we would beat Marietta. We practiced it all week.

Game night, and the stadium was filled. Marietta's quarterback, Bill Whetsell, scored first with just five minutes gone. We scored on a broken play and then on a 70-yard bust by Jerry Betts, the fastest guy on our team. Marietta came right back and scored. We were tied. But they had to kick off.

I called for "the play." Everything had to be perfect. Most important, the ball had to be kicked deep enough for Jerry Betts to get to it. All of Marietta was looking at Jerry—and all of Marietta would be after him if he caught the ball. He did. And then we went into action. Paul Franks took the ball in full sprint—he'd tied little bells to his shoelaces, and they tinkled as he ran past us. (Any time I feel a little down, I think about those jingling bells and magically feel better.) It was 90 yards of pure and utter perfection.

The second half was as close to warfare as you will find, without the bullets. Both teams went up

and down the field—but not into the end zones. Our fullback, Tom Chappelear, was on a mission. He ran with a pure passion that I would never see again for the rest of my career. Chappelear carried the ball 34 times—24 in the second half. No one carried into the end zone. The final score: 22–20, Cambridge.

Being new to the school, I didn't know the history of Tom Chappelear. Tom's father had graduated from Marietta College. A year earlier, just before the Marietta game, Tom's father had passed away from brain cancer. Tom was not playing for Cambridge or for me. Tom was playing for his father.

Jerry Betts is gone; in my mind, Paul Franks is still running up the sideline, bells tinkling. Tom Chappelear became a successful head coach at Cambridge High School. The game ball from that winning night is still in the school's trophy case.

ROY E. AULT ENGLEWOOD, FL

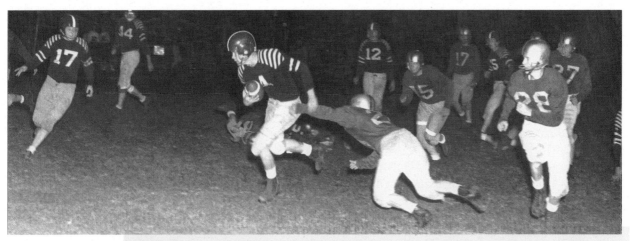

★ Larry managed to sneak in most of a football season, until one big play made it onto the local sports page.

THE ONLY ONE WHO COULD STOP HIM ON THE GRIDIRON WAS MOM

MY SOPHOMORE YEAR OF HIGH SCHOOL in Webster City, Iowa, I made the junior varsity team as a starting right halfback. But I knew there was no way Mom would sign off on my playing football: When I was 11, I was in bed for months with rheumatic fever. The doctor said I'd never be able to play sports or exert myself because of heart damage. So I forged her signature.

One of five kids in the family—out of an eventual eight—I was able to play most of the season without my parents noticing. Then in the next-to-last game of the season, *The Daily Freeman-Journal* ran a picture of me making a long run. Mom saw it, and that was the end of my football career.

LARRY PREHM FORT LAUDERDALE, FL

═══ ★ ★ ★ ═══

IT'S THE HALFTIME SHOW!

The Musical Majorettes performed to a sold-out crowd on Sept. 6, 1946, when the Cleveland Browns hosted the Miami Seahawks (I'm second from the right). Before pro football had cheerleaders, we played instruments, sang, did intricate marching routines and had good looks. It was a once-in-a-lifetime experience.

ELVIRA LAUSCHE FLYNN
WILLOUGHBY HILLS, OH

PICTURES FROM THE PAST
★★★ For the Win! ★★★

AFTERGLOW

The Chicago Bears won the National Football League championship game against the New York Giants at the Polo Grounds in New York on Dec. 15, 1946. Earlier that day, a failed bribery attempt was announced. Two Giants players were eventually suspended. "Papa Bear" George Halas (center back, waving) was the Bears' owner and coach, Sid Luckman (42) was the quarterback, and Dante Magnani (3) was a defensive back in the 24-14 win.

FUN THROUGH THE AGES

Here are my maternal grandmother, Lilly Hurt (second from top right), and her Oklahoma high school basketball teammates after they won the Corn Championship in 1920. I believe she's about 15 in this picture. She wasn't tall, so I'm guessing that back then, whoever tried out made the team!

ANDREA TAZELAAR CRYSTAL, MN

"COME ON, O-HI-O!"
The Ohio State University cheer squad leads the crowd at a 1960 football game in the "Buckeye Battle Cry."

THE CHAMPIONS

The 1952–'53 season was a winning one for our eighth grade basketball team at St. Rita Grammar School (now St. Rita of Cascia) on the South Side of Chicago, Illinois. I'm number 28 at top left.

BILL RUZGIS LONG BEACH, CA

EYES ON THE BALL

Football was king in Steelton, Pennsylvania, where many players from our small school made All-American. On a rainy Saturday in the fall of 1958, our Steel-High Steamrollers (white) run a pass play against Harrisburg's John Harris High School. I'm No. 28 at the far left.

JOHN BECK HARRISBURG, PA

Suzanne practices a spin whether onlookers are watching or not.

THE TIME OF HER LIFE ON THE ICE

ICE SKATING BROUGHT MANY YEARS OF JOY.

Mom felt that ice skates should run large and bought me a pair that were 1½ inches too long. I stuffed the long, narrow skates with Kleenex in the toe to fill the open space. She dropped me off at Brady's Pond on Staten Island, saying, "I'll be back in two hours to pick you up."

Bundled in leggings and sweaters, with plaid wool scarf flowing, I skated around the shallow area. When the temperature fell below freezing for several weeks, skaters also ventured onto the larger, deeper portion, joining a flotilla of ice sailboats.

The skates lasted throughout my childhood as I did my own version of spins, spirals and shoot-the-duck, a trick involving speed, crouching, extending one leg frontward and yelling, "Look out!"

Mom later confided she regretted not giving me skating lessons, as this was a sport I clearly loved.

Per tradition, my family ventured into New York City the day after Thanksgiving to see the Rockettes and the Christmas show at Radio City Music Hall. We walked across the street to view the skaters at Rockefeller Center, all skating in one big circle. Occasionally someone would break into spins and jumps in the eye of the circle, with spectators hoping of seeing something spectacular.

Years later, as a 20-something living on the Upper East Side, I took my long skates, which now almost fit, to Rockefeller Center's ice rink. I felt I was onstage. Joining the circle of skaters, I broke into the middle with a meek half-circle "spin." I'm sure the people looking from above expected something grand and didn't give my little spin a second nod.

Later, I moved to Anchorage, Alaska, with my husband, Don, and 3-year-old daughter, Sabrina, and it seemed to be the ice-skating capital of the world! Don created an ice rink in our backyard, shoveling snow to form solid banks and hosing it down every night to smooth the surface for our after-dinner family skate. And then my mother's wish for skating lessons finally came true.

Sabrina and I discovered an indoor rink that offered "mom and tot" weekday morning skate lessons. While the tots played duck, duck, goose on skates at one end, five of us moms learned front and backward crossovers, how to skate on inner and outer edges (which I never really mastered), spirals, and a three turn. For me, the three turn was big. The move is used by the real pros right before they lift off into their triple jumps. Mastering this maneuver gave me instant professional status. However, I feared what was to come next—the jump!—and quit taking lessons. Being 41 years old and four months pregnant (with Kalisa) served me well as an excuse.

SUZANNE G. BEYER BOTHELL, WA

FRIDAY NIGHT LIGHTS

THE ROLLER RINK WAS THE PLACE TO BE OR BE SEEN.

Friday nights in the early '40s you'd find me with my sisters, Betty and Bernice, and most of our friends at the Silver Lake Beach Roller Rink. It was a former dance hall converted to a roller rink. Inside was a long oval space for skating, with a section along one side for spectators. You always checked that section first to see who was there before buying a ticket.

The rink was surrounded by a waist-high wooden partition—just the right height to grab if you were unsteady on your skates.

Overhead was a big revolving light, and the music was always loud. There were a couple of fellows who skated backward and watched for falls or people going too fast. They also announced different types of skates. Most of the time, it was an "all skate." But there were also specials, like couples only, trios, waltzes and ladies' choice. The girls always liked that one.

The trios were fun, and so were the waltzes (especially when I finally learned to skate backward). One song I remember was the "Blue Skirt Waltz." When the lights dimmed, it almost felt as if you were floating along—with your best beau, of course.

We also went to the rink on Sunday nights. In fact, it was there on Dec. 7, 1941, that I first heard about Pearl Harbor. Things changed after that. So many of the young men went into the U.S. armed forces—and who wants to waltz with your sister?

BEATRICE COULTER OCONOMOWOC, WI

WATCHING ROLLER DERBY WAS A THRILL

SHE BECAME A FAST FAN OF THE LOS ANGELES BRAVES.

I n 1955, I was first introduced to Roller Derby. We had recently moved to San Diego, and as an avid roller skater, I was naturally attracted to the sport. We could watch the Los Angeles Braves only on KTLA, channel 5 in Los Angeles. Our TV had an antenna on the roof that rose to about 20 inches. If the weather was just right, we could catch glimpses of the games. If it wasn't, then all we got was the sound, and snow on the screen. Every Monday night—weather permitting—I was glued to the TV, watching Mary Youpelle, Russ Masro, Julie Patrick and all the other Braves.

After I joined the Mary Youpelle fan club, I started wearing an L.A. Braves team jacket just about everywhere I went. One time, I actually got to go to the Memorial Coliseum in Los Angeles to watch them in person. And when they traveled to San Diego, I would root for them at Lane Field, an outdoor baseball park that hosted the San Diego Padres. I was in seventh heaven when I could see them in person.

Finally, San Diego got its own team, the San Diego Clippers, and we got to see Roller Derby in person just about any time we wanted. Even though we had our own team, my heart still belonged to the Braves.

I dreamed of becoming a skater for many years, but it never materialized. Since the banked track looked like a big challenge, I joined a rexing club called the Imperial Rexers, which skated backward at the roller rink in Imperial Beach, California. I met many good friends there—and that satisfied my need to skate, which was in my blood.

VELMA STARMAN WHITTINGHAM TUCSON, AZ

BERT WALL

ROLLER SERIES 31 DERBY

Velma, a Roller Derby aficionado, got the program at right from a memorable event she attended.

OFFICIAL PROGRAM 25¢

LIFE ON THE STREET

ACTIVITIES CHANGED WITH THE SEASONS, BUT THERE WAS ALWAYS SOMETHING TO DO ON THIS BLOCK.

The block of 74th Street between Park Avenue and Broadway in North Bergen, New Jersey, was home to dozens of kids in the late 1950s. I was one of those 74th Street boys.

Some kids had nicknames—Duke, Chunky Broadway, Big Barrel and Little Barrel (no relation) and Hefty, who devoured 70 White Castle hamburgers at one sitting, according to the local legend.

In the spring, the car-lined street was filled with kids and their yo-yos—Duncans only—and a cavalcade of roller skates, bicycles and peach crate scooters. The crates doubled as display stands for periodically selling one's used comic books.

In summer, the freshly tarred street was a playground for ballgames: stick, whiffle and foot.

Smaller kids played box ball against the apartment buildings. In the fall, tops buzzed in the street, some wielding sharp nails. And, of course, in winter snowballs flew and kids made sidewalk igloos.

Most kids carried decks of cards, Bee or Bicycle, in their back pockets. Board games were relegated to the indoors, where playing pieces wouldn't get lost or blown away.

As we got older, working papers and driver's licenses signaled a change in status. People moved away and were soaked up by the suburbs, college or the military.

The oak with a gaping hole, perfectly sized for little kids to wriggle into, was torn out, replaced with a row of thin apple blossom trees.

GARY MIELO NEWTON, NJ

★★★ OLD GLORY ★★★

I took this shot on July 4, 1959, when a neighbor suggested staging an
Iwo Jima-inspired flag raising. From left are Bill Evans; John Price;
my husband, Charles; and John's sister Martha.

BARBARA HOWELL COLLINGSWOOD, NJ

ICONIC SIGHTS

Have you cruised Route 66, explored the Grand Canyon or seen St. Louis from the Gateway Arch? Let these stories take you across this great land.

Mickey Mouse, far left, greets a young visitor to Disneyland in 1968, the 40th anniversary of his creation; tourists take in Niagara Falls around 1967; below, the Space Needle commands the World's Fair in Seattle in 1962; and three women imitate Liberty holding her torch at New York's Ellis Island around 1950.

Mount Rushmore as it looks today. ★

CARVING MOUNT RUSHMORE

FAMILY BROUGHT DAD LUNCH AS HE WORKED WITH THE PRESIDENTS.

In 1935, my father became a carver of granite presidents in the Black Hills of South Dakota.

The Bell Telephone Co. in Rapid City had just laid off my dad, George Rumple, when a miner friend asked him if he'd be interested in working on the Mount Rushmore monument. It was the Great Depression, and my father, who had a wife and three kids to support, jumped at the chance.

Gutzon Borglum, the great man of the mountain and the chief sculptor, asked my dad if he had any experience with such a project. He was hired to do some work on the road leading up to the mountain and did well. Borglum promoted him to work on the grand project.

Dad's records show that he made anywhere from 50 cents an hour as a laborer, in 1936, to $1.25 an hour as a foreman and then a carver from 1936 to 1941.

When I was just 4 years old, in 1936, I heard my parents talk about the more than 750 stairs the workers had to climb. I recall going with my mother, Gladys, to take lunch to my dad on the top of Mount Rushmore. We'd sometimes walk up the many steps or ride up in a hoist "bucket."

I also met Chief Black Horse and Ben Black Elk, who smoked a peace pipe at the top of the mountain to ensure no harm would come to the almost 400 workers on the project. They let me try the pipe, but I didn't actually smoke it! No one died during the 14-year project, which ran from 1927 to 1941.

My father told me he worked on the eyes of Thomas Jefferson and on the facial features of Abraham Lincoln. He even gave George Washington a haircut.

Maxine's father, George Rumple (on the right in photo at left), and other men worked in hanging "cages" while bringing rock to life; a peace pipe used by Chief Black Horse (below, on the left) and Ben Black Elk, who posed with George, was intended to ensure the workers' safety; George Washington's head takes shape; and Maxine poses with her parents. ★

After dynamiting strategic spots, the workers used drills and jackhammers to create holes in the granite for easier carving. I remember hearing the explosions and seeing the white clouds of dust from the blasts.

I also recall President Franklin D. Roosevelt coming to see the mountain in 1936 for the dedication of the Thomas Jefferson head.

Nearby Keystone is where my brothers, Glen and Lyle, and I attended school. When work ended on the project in 1941, we moved to the state of Washington and then to California.

Standing on the top of Mount Rushmore is still an awesome memory for me, and Dad always referred to the Mount Rushmore memorial as the "No. 1 wonder of the world."

MAXINE EVANS MANTECA, CA

MY FATHER TOLD ME HE WORKED ON THE EYES OF THOMAS JEFFERSON AND ON THE FACIAL FEATURES OF ABRAHAM LINCOLN. HE EVEN GAVE GEORGE WASHINGTON A HAIRCUT.

★

TRAVELS WITH AUNT RIDGELY

INTREPID VIRGINIAN MARVELS AT 1930s AMERICA.

A girls' road trip is pretty common today, but during the 1930s, when cars were still a luxury and women didn't have as much freedom, it was rare. But my Aunt Ridgely wasn't exactly an average woman.

Born Elizabeth Ridgely Jackson in 1898, she was the second youngest of 11 children and the only one in the family to graduate from high school. Later, she earned a college degree in an era when few women even wanted one, much less had the opportunity to obtain one.

Aunt Ridgely insisted on good manners and behavior, but she also had a wonderful sense of humor and a keen curiosity about other cultures. So it's no surprise that in 1938, at age 41, she traveled across the United States with five of her friends: Grace Clevinger, Mamie Childs, Ada Woore, Annie Reese and Carrie Cochran.

Recently we found the map and a portion of her trip journal, which had been stored away since her death in 1983. According to the newspaper clipping tucked inside the log, the group left Winchester, Virginia, on July 5 in a Buick touring car driven by Carrie's nephew Thomas.

Entries documenting the first part of the trip have been lost, but we know that on July 20 they were in Pasadena, California, where they drove down Orange Grove Avenue, "the street on which the most millionaires live." They saw actors' mansions along Hollywood and Sunset boulevards and took in a concert at the Hollywood Bowl under "the starry dome of the sky."

Sunsets at Grand Canyon National Park were a revelation. In wonder, the travelers saw "the blue change into purple and back to blue and then to gray, as the sun slipped down behind the rim,

illuminating the colors of the canyon walls. We came away feeling that never again would we look upon such a beautiful sight."

She had lunch at Bright Angel campground on Aug. 2. Aunt Ridgely also took a mule tour down into the canyon, though there is no mention of it in her diary.

She often spoke of that mule ride, her eyes widening as she remembered her terror at looking down the sheer cliffs.

Continuing their drive through Arizona, and despite the heat of the desert in August in a car with no air conditioning, the travelers remained enthralled. Ridgely had a hard time "staying on the straight and narrow," resisting the urge to take a piece of the Petrified Forest with her. In the Painted Desert, she bought me a beautiful sand painting.

The group soaked up Navajo culture from Gallup to Santa Fe along Route 66 in New Mexico, but when they reached Taos, the Buick, which they called Barney, needed repair.

Climbing Pikes Peak, at an elevation of 14,115 feet, was a challenge in the struggling Buick: "Breathlessly, we watched the mileposts as we slowly passed around the curves. In a little while, Barney was hot, so we stopped to rest him."

Ridgely saw "more beautiful wildflowers than in any other state" west of Denver, but on the eastern stretch of Colorado, there was ample evidence of

---

CLIMBING PIKES PEAK, AT AN ELEVATION OF 14,115 FEET, WAS A CHALLENGE IN THE STRUGGLING BUICK.

★

---

drought and poverty brought on by the Dust Bowl and Great Depression.

As the Virginians wound through the Allegheny Mountains and coal mines of West Virginia, they were impatient to get home. No sight was as sublime to them as the Virginia state line.

"Our most efficient driver ... had safely taken us over 7,977 miles of hot plains, steep mountains and dry deserts; through windstorms, sandstorms and rainstorms; through heat and cold, over good roads and bad, back to the Garden Spot of the World. Our memories of scenes and pleasures will stay with us as long as we live."

I loved her stories about this trip and shared her passion for seeing new vistas. In my life, I lived in Hawaii, California and Connecticut, covering thousands of miles across this great nation, before finally settling in Vermont.

I savored every view because of Aunt Ridgely's descriptions of her own travels.

LOUISE KLEH SOUTH BURLINGTON, VT

Ridgely Jackson wrote with verve in her travel journal (top left) of the 1938 road trip with her friends, which included a stop at Yosemite National Park (left); Above, Ridgely holds Louise's daughter Cindy in 1959. Louise is on the far right beside her mother.

THE GREAT GRAND CANYON

COUNTRY'S GEOLOGICAL WONDER HAS BEEN A NATIONAL PARK FOR MORE THAN 100 YEARS.

T rue to its name, Grand Canyon National Park is anything but small. With more than 1 million acres along the 18-mile-wide gap from the North Rim to the South Rim, the canyon in northwest Arizona inspires all who peer over its edges. On Feb. 26, 1919, President Woodrow Wilson signed into law an act of Congress establishing Grand Canyon National Park, which soon became a popular attraction. In tribute to this beacon of the all-American road trip, backdrop of family snapshots and symbol of the nation's adventurous spirit, we look at moments in its past.

BY **RACHAEL LISKA**

Early History

Tribal peoples, including Havasupai (above), Hualapai, Navajo and Hopi, flourish in and around the canyon. At least 11 tribes are connected to the area today.

1869
One-armed Civil War veteran John Wesley Powell leads nine men into the canyon via the Colorado River in the earliest recorded visit by nonnatives. Only six men complete the journey.

1908
President Theodore Roosevelt makes the Grand Canyon a national monument. "Let this great wonder of nature remain as it now is," he declares. "You cannot improve on it. But what you can do is keep it for your children, your children's children, and all who come after you, as the one great sight which every American should see."

1922
Phantom Ranch is built under the direction of architect Mary Elizabeth Jane Colter (above). The historic oasis is the only lodging below the canyon rim and is built from wood and native stone. Nestled beside Bright Angel Creek, it can be reached only via mule, on foot or by water.

1928
President Calvin Coolidge approves construction of Boulder Dam (now Hoover Dam). Completed in 1936, it was the world's largest hydroelectric dam and concrete structure.

1937
Haldene "Buzz" Holmstrom makes the first solo trip down the Green and Colorado rivers and through Grand Canyon in a handmade rowboat, traveling 1,100 miles in 52 days.

1956
Two planes maneuver to avoid storm clouds and collide midair over the Grand Canyon, claiming 128 lives. The accident helps spur public outcry for tighter flight rules, leading to the Federal Aviation Act.

1971
The Brady Bunch opens its third season with a trip to the Grand Canyon. The three-part episode has several cliffhangers—amid the actual cliffs—that include the family getting locked in a jail cell, and losing Bobby and Cindy on a canyon trail.

1985
State Route 67, the sole access to the canyon's North Rim, is designated an Arizona State Scenic Road and National Forest Scenic Byway. Open for only five months from spring to autumn, the highway is buried under more than 9 feet of snow during winter.

1991
Captive-bred California condors are released to the wild after the species is rescued from near extinction. The first egg from a reintroduced condor is laid in Grand Canyon National Park.

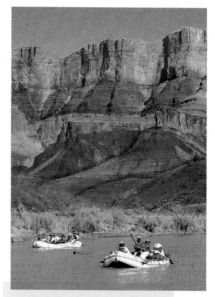

The Colorado River carved the Grand Canyon more than 6 million years ago. Today some 20,000 people ride its rushing waters past the canyon's walls. ★

California-bound, Bob and Florence take a break during their epic journey to get dolled up and climb mountains in the Southwest. ★

THE AMERICAN DREAM ALONG ROUTE 66

TRAVELING THE MOTHER OF ALL ROADS.

Bob Snow and I married in 1945, shortly after we both were discharged from the military in Illinois. He had been an aircraft crew chief during the war and loved it, so he hoped to do the same kind of work in peacetime. His dream was to apply to the Flying Tigers, the country's first cargo freight airline, which was in California.

I was in love and would have gone to the moon with him, but California? That was beyond my imagination. It became very real in 1946 when we bought a Kozy Coach house trailer and outfitted

it with birch cupboards, sink, water pump, refrigerator and space heater. Loaded, the thing had to weigh 1½ tons.

"Now we can go to California!" Bob exclaimed. So we hitched the coach to our 1940 Plymouth coupe and headed west out of Chicago along Route 66.

In Missouri, we passed several handmade signs: See the Cave. These led us to an old farmhouse, where two elderly ladies welcomed us like old friends. They took turns explaining the natural formations in the cave and shooing away bats, saying, "Don't scare the nice folks!"

The Oklahoma oil wells we saw were an ugly part of the scenery for me, a farm girl raised in the green rolling hills of southwest Michigan.

Texas and New Mexico rolled by. In each little town we saw hotels, stores and gas stations in unusual styles, including teepees, pueblos and frontierlike storefronts. We'd stop nightly at a gas station, where for $5 or $10, we could plug into the electricity, fix our food, use the bathroom and bathe out of a basin. It was a simple, easy life.

In Flagstaff, Arizona, we left the trailer at a gas station to drive

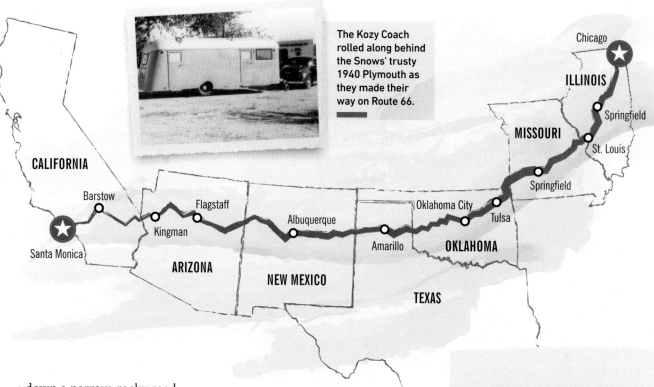

The Kozy Coach rolled along behind the Snows' trusty 1940 Plymouth as they made their way on Route 66.

CALIFORNIA

Barstow

Santa Monica

Kingman

Flagstaff

ARIZONA

NEW MEXICO

Albuquerque

Amarillo

TEXAS

OKLAHOMA

Oklahoma City

Tulsa

Springfield

MISSOURI

St. Louis

Springfield

ILLINOIS

Chicago

down a narrow, rocky road to the Grand Canyon, which was breathtaking way beyond description. We happened to park near a couple from Galesburg, Michigan, and we all hugged as if we knew each other.

Up in the mountains, we passed several big cars on the side of the highway with radiators boiling over. Our coupe was performing beautifully, thanks to Bob, a top-notch mechanic who kept the Plymouth well-tuned. I was proud of him.

The mountain driving involved a lot of maneuvering around tight corners and up and down steep grades, but we finally reached the foothills, where we could see miles of flat road leading into Bakersfield, California. As we descended, we continued to gain speed, until I peeked at the dashboard and saw that we were going 82 mph.

I gripped Bob's arm. "I don't like to go this fast," I told him.

"I don't either," he said. "But we have no more brakes." We had to ride it out as best we could.

At the end of our journey we settled in at a Culver City trailer park. Bob worked for the Flying Tigers for several months until the company relocated to Burbank. We couldn't find a decent trailer park near there, so we moved on. We traveled as far as Oregon in hopes of finding another airline job for Bob before eventually deciding to head back home to Michigan.

After a terrifying haul east through the Rocky Mountains on switchback roads beside 6,000-foot drops, I'd had enough of that Kozy Coach. We wound up selling it in Reno, Nevada, to a couple that planned to take it to Alaska along the recently built Alcan Highway. I wished them good luck and blew a kiss goodbye to what had been our sweet little home for over a year. We'd seen a lot of the country together.

FLORENCE SNOW FINKEY
KALAMAZOO, MI

ROOTS OF ROUTE 66

America's very first fully paved highway has quite a storied history.

★ Lt. Edward Beale, head of the U.S. Army Camel Corps, surveyed part of the route in 1857.

★ Established in 1926, it covers 2,448 miles.

★ Cyrus Avery of Tulsa, OK, oilman and loyal 66 booster, nicknamed it the Main Street of America.

★ An early 66 publicity stunt was the Bunion Derby, a 1928 footrace from California to New York. Cherokee runner Andy Hartley Payne won the $25,000 prize.

★ John Steinbeck called it "the mother road" in *The Grapes of Wrath*, his 1939 chronicle of Dust Bowl migrants.

★ It was decertified in 1985, but about 85% is still drivable.

★ Roy's Cafe and Motel in Amboy, CA. is one of the most recognizable sights along old U.S. 66. Built in 1938 and expanded in the '50s, Roy's angled storefront and Googie-style sign have been in many films and TV shows.

RAISED ON THE ROAD

ROUTE 66 IS TRULY MY MOTHER ROAD. I grew up in Fontana, then Azusa, and as an adult, I lived in Glendora—all on Route 66 in California. I married my husband, Ted, in 1960 at St. Frances of Rome Church on Route 66 in Azusa. It's still there and always packed on Sundays. Throughout the '60s and '70s, I worked at several businesses along Route 66, including a thrift store, a grocery, a boat dealer and the Foothill Drive-In Theatre in Azusa. They've all closed, although the marquee at the drive-in is intact and the site is sometimes used for special events.

I might add that I got my only traffic violation on Route 66. The officer who issued me the ticket turned out to be one of my neighbors.

KAREN MEYERS TWENTYNINE PALMS, CA

A TIMELY TRIP

MAKING A MEMORABLE JOURNEY TO FIRST JOB.

Setting out bright and early that day in February 1964, I was eager to begin my trip west. I had just graduated from Purdue University and looked forward to driving a new blue Ford Fairlane 500—my graduation present—from my home in Rockville, Indiana, to California, where I'd accepted a job.

In St. Louis, Missouri, I lost sight of the other car I'd been traveling with while navigating the construction zone around the base of the Jefferson National Expansion Memorial—now known as the Gateway Arch—which wouldn't be completed until the next year. I was relieved to be on my own; now I could drive without the constant worry of keeping another car in my rearview mirror.

On day three, I got to Flagstaff, Arizona, about 5 p.m., checked into a little motel and settled in to wait out a snowstorm. The next morning there were at least 10 cars in the ditch within the first few miles. I cruised on by, glad those Hoosier blizzards had taught me something about how and when to drive in bad weather.

> I REACHED PASADENA, CALIFORNIA, AS THE SUN SET, THE VALLEY BEFORE ME AN EXPANSE OF MULTICOLORED LIGHTS.
> ★

I reached Pasadena, California, as the sun set, the valley before me an expanse of multicolored lights. Never before had I seen anything so exotic—it struck fear into the heart of this Indiana farm girl.

But it was a good kind of fear, for California was my land of promise: My solo flight along the Mother Road had brought me to the home of Douglas Aircraft, where the next week I would start my career as an engineer in the science and space division.

SHARLIE WOIWOD ARVADA, CO

Blue Swallow Motel, still family-owned, has been a fixture in Tucumcari, NM, since the 1940s. Retro enthusiasts love its pink stucco exterior, period furnishings and groovy neon sign.

★ Fishing Bridge in Yellowstone has drawn tourists for decades.

THE BRIDGE TO FUN AND FRIENDSHIPS

EARNING MONEY IN A SPECTACULAR SETTING.

During the summers of 1970 and '71, I worked as a seasonal employee at Yellowstone National Park. I applied to work there after a friend told me she had applied to work at Glacier National Park. Coincidentally, I got the job and she did not.

At the time, I lived in Minneapolis and could take the train to just outside the park. The day I arrived in early June, I wore a sleeveless sundress and sandals, only to find snow on the ground. I had to change clothes immediately.

I was assigned to work at Fishing Bridge, an area that, along with the bridge built in 1937, included cabins, a campground, a cafeteria, boat rentals, a service station and more. I worked in the cafeteria six days a week. During my off-hours, I hitchhiked around the park with other employees but accepted rides only from families with kids. We met a lot of nice park visitors that way.

> WORKING AT YELLOWSTONE BROADENED MY HORIZONS AND INTRODUCED ME TO A VARIETY OF PEOPLE AND EXPERIENCES.
> ★

Another activity I decided to try was joining Yellowstone's Christmas in August choir. Employees learned Handel's *Messiah* and sang to visitors at locations all over the park. I'm not much of a singer—my range consists of five notes and three of them are flat—but the prospect of camaraderie, and four days off with pay, was worth it.

Working at Yellowstone broadened my horizons and introduced me to a variety of people and experiences. Dave and Kayla, a couple who went to school at Westminster Choir College in New Jersey; Diane Zvolena, a teacher from Wisconsin; Becky Strong from Colorado; a gal named Vi; and a guy who went by Bonko all made it memorable.

Some were away from home for the first time and reveled in their freedom. Others were more conservative. But each one helped me mature.

JOY AXT PELLA, IA

VACATION TIME!

Americans have long had the urge to roam and discover new sights both near and far.

Ready to Relax

It's hard to say who's having more fun in this Hertz rental car ad, the bathers or the car. The scene shows Nevada's now defunct Desert Inn resort in Las Vegas.

SEE MORE...DO MORE...
HAVE MORE FUN! THE
Hertz Rent A Car Way!

Nevada's largest and most deluxe resort hotel, Wilbur Clark's beautiful Desert Inn, in Las Vegas. With its more than 270 acres and Olympic-sized pool, the Desert Inn affords the traveler all that he might want in sport, recreation, and just plain relaxation.

Hertz rental rates are reasonable ... whether you drive a Hertz car from home to vacation spot, or travel by plane or train and have a Hertz car waiting at your destination. Your car can be reserved in advance by the Hertz office in your home city. For example, this is what it will cost you for a clean new Ford Fordomatic or other fine car in Las Vegas, Nevada. For driving 300 miles in a week—going wherever, whenever you want—you will pay only $64.00!

If there are five riding, the cost is reduced to $13.00 a person. (Rates vary slightly in different cities. Convertible rates are slightly higher.) And Hertz furnishes all gasoline, oil ... and proper insurance for the entire rental period ... at no extra cost!

HERTZ SERVICE: *what it is and how to get it...*

ply look in your telephone directory under "H" for nearest Hertz office. Show your driver's license and r identification at the office and off you go in a car ate as your own. Rent for an hour, day, week or It's as easy as checking into your hotel.

e entire rental period, Hertz furnishes all gaso- ... Public Liability, Property Damage, Fire and rance, and $100.00 deductible collision protection xtra cost! If you pay for additional gasoline or oil ip, Hertz will reimburse you for the full amount.

re of a Hertz car locally or in another city, ervation in advance. Any Hertz office will make

one for you, anywhere, for any time. Always insist on Hertz!

Hertz Rent A Car Service is available at nearly 900 offices in over 550 cities throughout the world. For your convenience, Hertz issues Charge Cards to qualified individuals and firms, and honors Air Travel and Rail Credit Cards.

Additional Information—call your nearest Hertz office or—write or phone Hertz Rent A Car System, Department 885, 218 South Wabash Avenue, Chicago 4, Illinois. Phone: WEbster 9-5165.

TZ *Rent A Car* **SYSTEM**

Now serving you in more than 550 cities in the United States, Canada, Alaska, Mexico, Hawaii, New Zealand, Cuba, Haiti, Puerto Rico, Jamaica, the Virgin Islands, Great Britain, Ireland, France, Belgium, Holland and Switzerland.

'55

THINGS LOOK BRIGHT ALL OVER WITH THAT

GOLDEN
Florida
GLOW!

A fabulous state of well-being...
which makes everything
seem bright and shining
...and *extra special!*

From border to border, Florida's packed with one of the world's great concentrations of fun facilities ... added to world-famed climate and amazing natural wonders... at rates to make your vacation budget smile and s-t-r-e-t-c-h!

FOR A VACATION...OR FOREVER!
No wonder some 5 million Americans will holiday in Florida this year ... that over a million have settled here *for good* in the past ten years. That's convincing evidence Florida's not for a gilt-edged few ... but for *everyone!* Want details? Mail the coupon!

HERE'S HEALTH! DRINK A GLASS OF FLORIDA SUNSHINE EVERY DAY!

STATE OF FLORIDA
1303-L COMMISSION BLDG., TALLAHASSEE, FLA.

Name
Address
City _____ Zone __ State

FABULOUS FLORIDA...WARM in Winter—COOL in Summer!

'54

Blue Skies

Florida is touted here as a place for the whole family, with warm temps and palm trees swaying in the breeze. Who can beat the slogan "Fabulous Florida...warm in winter—cool in summer!"

HEADED WEST IN A SOUPED-UP MODEL T

IT WOULD HAVE BEEN SEEN as a daring venture in 1916 to travel from Madison, Wisconsin, to Yellowstone National Park. But that is just what my grandparents Herman and Agnes Licht did for their honeymoon. My grandfather fashioned a camper onto their Model T, and Agnes kept a diary of their adventures, mentioning numerous tire punctures, muddy roads and trails. Along the first leg of their journey, they got permission from farmers to stay overnight in their fields—long before the days of commercial campgrounds.

Getting into Yellowstone was an adventure in itself. They took a train that left Ipswich, South Dakota, at 6:45 a.m. and got into Gardiner, Montana, at 10 the next morning. From Gardiner and within the park, visitors traveled on horse-powered coaches. Agnes and Herman stayed six days in a "tent cabin," a small building with wood slats on the lower half and canvas covering the top half. The park service provided a bed, a table with candles, a stove, a washstand and a couple of chairs. All visitors ate in a communal dining tent.

Their experiences during that trip more than 100 years ago, along with my grandmother's diary, are a beloved part of our family history.

SHIRLEY ROECKER REEDSBURG, WI

ON PATROL AS A PARK RANGER

DURING THE SUMMERS OF 1968 AND 1969, I had the good fortune to be a seasonal National Park Service ranger in Glacier National Park in northwest Montana. It was a slice of heaven.

After I got my bachelor's degree from the University of South Dakota, I was assigned to combat infantry units in Vietnam for 14 months. Back home, I met Judy, a student at USD, and we got married in May 1972. That summer, I went back to the park service, but this time I was assigned to Yellowstone in Wyoming. A major part of a ranger's job was protecting visitors from thermal areas, bear and bison encounters, and accidents on rocky cliffs or twisting park roads.

On my days off, Judy and I spent our honeymoon summer soaking up all the beauty of Yellowstone. We fished for trout, hiked the trails, admired the elk herds in the Swan Lake Flats and, once, flew around the park in a helicopter with a neighbor who was a contract pilot.

I still have the ranger uniform that I wore from 1968 to 1973. Judy and I have many treasured memories of the days when I was privileged to be a Yellowstone "Smokey."

PATRICK MURPHY SIOUX FALLS, SD

Newlyweds Judy and Patrick spent their first summer together exploring Yellowstone in 1972. ★

My wife, Shirley, and me at the Yosemite tunnel overlook, 1987. ★

COUPLE'S FAVORITE PLACE

I GREW UP IN SOUTHERN CALIFORNIA, where the mountains and the beach are short drives away. I had joined the Boy Scouts especially to go camping, so I was eager to visit Yosemite when I was 17 years old. I was not prepared for what met my eyes. The first sight to greet me took my breath away. The whole valley opens up before you: El Capitan, Bridalveil Fall, and, in the distance, Half Dome. With my church group, I hiked the trails, swam in and tubed down the snow-fed river, and watched the "fire fall" from Glacier Point.

Years later, in 1962, I married my college sweetheart, and we spent our honeymoon in Yosemite that April. We were almost snowed in! We went back many times. I've visited lots of our national parks, but my favorite is Yosemite. It was my wife's favorite place, too. We both really enjoyed seeing the beauty of God's creation.

HOWARD BOWMAN DUNCANVILLE, TX

INVASION OF THE COPPERHEADS!

MY DAD IS A FISHERIES BIOLOGIST, so my childhood was packed with trips to national parks across the country. During one of these trips, on day three of a hike through Great Smoky Mountains National Park, we found what to my 11-year-old brain was the perfect campsite. It was in a valley full of logs and trees and had plenty of room for our two tents. Our group was my mom and dad, my two sisters, a cousin and my uncle.

My uncle and I were arranging logs around the campfire when we found a displeased snake. My 16-year-old cousin identified it as a copperhead, so we knew that if we didn't bother it, it wouldn't bother us.

Within minutes, we'd spotted a second copperhead, and then another, and another—around 15 snakes in all! We wondered if we were on a migratory path or a nest, or if there was some weird snake dance going on. We thought removal was the best option, and the boys set to work finding Y-shaped branches for flinging the snakes away. But they just kept coming! An hour passed, and then, thankfully, the snakes dwindled to just a few. At bedtime, we huddled up and walked with two flashlights through our snake-infested campsite to the tents. I jumped on my dad's back, and we were spared.

TAYLOR YESS WINONA, MN

A MAGICAL TRAIN RIDE WITH MR. DISNEY

HE MADE A SPECIAL DAY EVEN MORE FANTASTIC.

I n 1955, Walt Disney was everything to a five-year-old. This was the man who'd brought us *20,000 Leagues Under the Sea* and that wonderful *Nautilus*. How could one person bring all of this to people our age? And to top it off, he was building an amusement park in California! As great as it sounded, Disneyland in California seemed as unreachable as nirvana to a little kid in Denison, Texas.

To my shock, Dad announced that we were going to the opening of Disneyland. It was too much for me to comprehend, but one morning, we were up before the sun and headed west.

The week after the VIP opening found us sitting in a vast parking lot with about a dozen cars scattered here and there. Eight o'clock came and went, and those of us in the lot just kept looking at one another. Nothing was happening.

Finally, someone came out and waved us through the entrance. I hit the ground running. From the minute we got inside, I was in a fantasyland. It was a living, breathing movie set, and I was right in the middle of it! Main Street led to a plaza with a futuristic clock that was so popular in the '50s. We walked down a lane with a river on our left and saw the large riverboat pull away. Just ahead was the princess's castle. I begged Dad to shoot everything with our Kodak Brownie.

Meanwhile, I was keeping an eye out for other surprises, and lo and behold, I saw him! There he was, sitting on a built-in bench, puffing on his pipe, and just looking around with this big grin on his face: the Walt Disney.

I couldn't approach him. That would be like approaching the Wizard of Oz, except Walt was real. After I pestered, my dad finally walked up and asked him, "Excuse me, but my son seems to think you're Walt Disney." Mr. Disney stood up, smiled, and

A photo was captured of Larry's mom, Larry and Walt Disney himself.

stretched out his hand. "Well, he's right. How do you like my park?" From then on, it was a blur. I shook his hand, and he said hello to my mother and older sister. I was too dazed to remember anything else for a while, but luckily we captured a photo of my mom, me and the man himself.

But it got better: As we stood in line to ride the real steam-engine train, Walt Disney walked up and asked Dad if it would be all right if I rode up in the engine cab with him. Dad said sure. It was Walt's train, after all! Mr. Disney slowly pushed the throttle forward, and the beautiful steam engine began to puff. I sat in Mr. Disney's lap, with my hand also on the throttle, as he pointed out things in the park he was particularly proud of getting finished before the opening. We made one complete circuit, and then Dad and I said our goodbyes to Walt Disney.

LARRY WILLIAMS TOMBALL, TX

PICTURES FROM THE PAST
★ ★ ★ Love of Disney ★ ★ ★

FREQUENT VISITOR

I grew up in Southern California, so I visited Disneyland a lot. These two photos are from a trip in 1974. My son Gary loved Winnie-the-Pooh! In the antique truck are my daughter Andrea, Gary and my husband.

SHIRLEY SCHUMAN
GLENDALE, AZ

TICKET TO RIDE

I grew up in Chowchilla, California, as one of five children. When Disneyland opened, you bought a ticket book from a booth near the entrance and used all your ride tickets for the day. This ticket book from the 1970s cost $5.45.

KELLI KILDAY REIMER FRESNO, CA

MEETING GOOFY!

In 1964, my sister, Elizabeth (right), and I met Goofy in Disneyland. Our mom had made us matching outfits so she could easily spot us in the crowd.

CAROLYN BERRY MacARTHUR DALLAS, GA

PICTURES FROM THE PAST
★ ★ ★ Travel Destinations ★ ★ ★

SUMMER SIGHTSEEING

In 1967, my parents took me and three friends on a trip to Philadelphia, Pennsylvania, to see the Liberty Bell, and Atlantic City, New Jersey, where we strolled on the old-fashioned boardwalk.

LINDA HUGHES QUINCY, IL

WILD WEST

I was a fifth grade teacher when I captured this photo of the bustling charm of Reno, Nevada, in 1952. An avid traveler and photographer, I spent my summers seeing the country and, later, many foreign lands.

VIRGINIA THURTLE EUCLID, OH

BUILDING A GATEWAY

Designed by Eero Saarinen in 1947 and dedicated in 1968, the 63-story-tall
Gateway Arch in St. Louis, MO, is part of a 91-acre national park and celebrates
the city's role as a gateway to the west in the 19th century. The park also has
a museum.

Bert wraps his arm around sister Muriel in 1943. Adventure could be found at the Long Beach Pike.

MEET AT THE PIKE

LASTING MEMORIES ARE BUILT FROM SIGHTS, SOUNDS AND SMELLS.

On a strip of ocean shore in Long Beach, California, stood the Long Beach Pike, an amusement zone that had started life as a wooden boardwalk connecting the Long Beach Pier to the Plunge bathhouse. The Pike was a place of enchantment in this city formerly known as Iowa by the Sea, and predated the splendor of Disneyland. Often, the last words my mother heard on Saturday morning as the screen door slammed were, "Mom, I'm going to the Pike."

As kids, we didn't yet realize that anticipation is the principal ingredient of a happy experience, but as we vigorously pedaled our Schwinn or Columbia bicycles to our ultimate goal, who cared? The Pike was our magnet and that was how we got there.

Passing through the arch below the Ocean Center Building, we finally were on the Pike and in kid heaven. My senses were immediately assailed with bright lights, rumbling thrill rides, bells, whistles and shouts from sideshow barkers, and the whoops and shrieks of people at play. Then came the heady aroma of buttery popcorn, saltwater taffy, roasting peanuts and sizzling hamburgers.

> AS KIDS, WE DIDN'T YET REALIZE THAT ANTICIPATION IS THE PRINCIPAL INGREDIENT OF A HAPPY EXPERIENCE...

I was a lucky kid with a quarter in my pocket. Most of the day I would be consumed with indecision about where to spend it, but I relished all the choices: a ride on the bumper cars or the Cyclone Racer or a stroll through the Laff in the Dark fun house.

The Pike taught me how to prioritize my spending and to develop a personal radar. As a youngster, I viewed the concessionaires and ride attendants as gods of pleasure. As I entered my teens, though, I gained a greater understanding of the Pike's world around me.

Begun as a beach and bathhouse in 1902, the Pike closed in 1979. Having once enjoyed its hospitality, I feel the same tug each time I'm hit with the zesty aroma from a hot dog stand or the squeals of children at play. Those sounds and smells trigger memories of long-past summer days and a hauntingly familiar voice that says, "Mom, I'm going to the Pike."

BERT ANDERSON HEMET, CA

★ ★ ★ OCEAN BREEZE ★ ★ ★

We loved to take annual jaunts with our daughters Ann and Lani.
In 1964, we stopped in beautiful Monterey on California's central coast.

MERRY FLANAGAN ST. PAUL, MN

MADE IN THE USA

American products and fashions that speak to
our innovative spirit. The new technology can be
exciting, and sometimes colorful!

At far left, the first Corvettes roll off the assembly line at the Chevy plant in Flint, MI, in 1953. The cars originally sold for $3,250. Rock and roll pioneer Chuck Berry struts his signature duck walk with his Gibson at a 1980 concert in Hollywood, CA. Below, stunt rider Evel Knievel pops a wheelie on his Harley-Davidson around 1975.

Atomic style furnishings recall the essence of Lustron living in a restored model in Indianapolis. ★

MIDCENTURY METAL

VINTAGE LUSTRON HOME HAS STAYING POWER.

ustron homes occupy a special niche in America's post–World War II housing story. GIs returned from overseas to a significant housing shortage, which was the result of a serious building slowdown in the preceding decades. Few could afford to build new homes during the Great Depression; in WWII, materials that would've been used for housing went to the war effort instead.

So what were young veterans and their new spouses to do? Many turned to prefabricated houses, with support from the government. Between 1945 and 1952, the Veterans Administration backed nearly 24 million home loans for returning vets. U.S. homeownership grew from 44% in 1940 to 62% in 1960.

Lustron homes came on the scene in the late 1940s. The brainchild of Chicago industrialist Carl G. Strandlund, the houses were composed of factory-made porcelain-over-steel panels and erected at the building site. Strandlund persuaded the government that his prefab houses would ease

Lustron exteriors came in delicate pastels, including yellow (above). A combination dishwasher/ washing machine was an option; all models included attractive storage, such as this bedroom unit.

Space-saving built-ins like the shelving unit dividing the kitchen and dining area were signature features of Lustrons. ★

a housing squeeze made worse by slow traditional construction methods. In 1946, he was offered a former defense plant, the 1 million-square-foot Curtiss-Wright aircraft building in Columbus, Ohio, to make his houses.

Under the Lustron slogan "a new standard for living," models went up in cities across the country. Lustron Corp. shipped the houses on custom trailers along with all the parts, down to the bolts—more than 3,000 pieces.

However, in-plant manufacturing and on-site construction processes were fraught with problems. Strandlund couldn't find a way to make money on the homes or pay back his substantial government

loans. The company went bankrupt and shut down in 1950.

Today, their distinctive appearance and their fascinating history make Lustrons a favorite among retro enthusiasts. Of the 2,680 Lustrons built, fewer than 1,200 remain. Several are in the Midwest. In Indianapolis, Lustron owner Kelly Huff spent months bringing hers back to its former glory. The photos on these pages showing the results of her efforts also make plain why cozy Lustrons were a popular housing choice at midcentury.

BY **NANCY A. HERRICK**

Decor in a restored Lustron combines period pieces with modern comforts, left and top; some original buyers added the upgrade of a breezeway with jalousie windows, above. ★

NEW STANDARD FOR LIVING

★ The original and most popular Lustron model was the Westchester. It had two bedrooms, one bath, kitchen, living room, dining room and utility area on a concrete slab. No basement, no attic.

★ Models shipped to 36 states, mainly in the Midwest and East Coast.

★ Originally Lustrons were priced at $7,500 to $8,000, but that price wasn't guaranteed.

★ By 1950, the price had increased to around $11,000. Lustron Corp. lost money on each home as it never reached its optimum of 700 a month.

★ It took up to 1,500 hours to erect the first houses. That number was later reduced to 250 to 350 hours—or two weeks.

★ Exteriors came in maize yellow, dove gray, surf blue and desert tan. Interiors were beige or gray.

★ Ads billed them as "fireproof, rustproof, decay-proof, termite-proof and rat-proof."

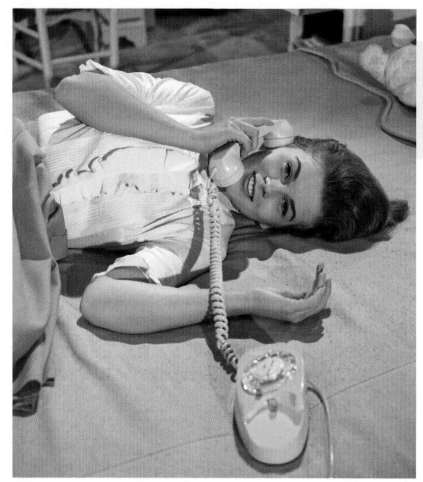

A PRINCESS IN EVERY HOME

THE SIXTIES CALLED—THEY WANT THEIR PHONE BACK.

D uring the late 1950s, in a bustling economy focused on youth culture, companies devoted a lot of research and development to products that appealed to our sense of fun.

The toy industry boomed, and the success of a new product usually depended on an elusive quality that was hard to measure, but we knew it when we saw it. Today, we might call it the cool factor. Wham-O's Frisbee ('57) and Hula Hoop ('58), Roller Derby's skateboard and Mattel's Barbie (both '59)—all had that special something in spades.

And so did the Princess phone.

Ma Bell was late to the party when it came to sexy products—with a monopoly on the phone business, it didn't have to finesse us—but the little oval gem that hit Bell's lineup in the fall of 1959 made up for lost time.

Made by Western Electric from a blueprint by leading industrial designer Henry Dreyfuss, the Princess had a slim profile and one-third the footprint of the standard desk phone—ideal for a bedside table. Its regal name was a direct appeal to teenage girls, a fact not lost on the filmmakers of teen romp *Bye Bye Birdie* (1963), who gave breakout star Ann-Margret an aqua blue Princess phone as a prop.

Here are more fun facts about the phone every girl wanted for Christmas.

BY **MARY-LIZ SHAW**

Pretty in Pastels

The Princess came in five colors: aqua blue, beige, pink, white and turquoise. After 1963, turquoise was available only on request and was discontinued in 1970. A lamp in the dial served as a night light; it glowed softly when the phone was not in use, brightly when the handset was off the hook.

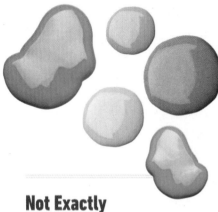

Not Exactly a Ringing Endorsement

Although instantly popular, the first Princess version had a few quirks that annoyed early adopters. Its housing was too small to fit an internal ringer—an external ringer was an add-on. The Princess required a special transformer for the light-up dial, and it was significantly lighter than the usual desk phone, which caused it to slide around as you dialed.

For Her

Advertising openly appealed to a feminine aesthetic. Early print spots for the Princess show women's hands reaching for the phone, with the slogan, "It's little! It's lovely! It lights!" Princess ads targeted both homemakers and businesses that catered to women, including salons, dress shops and jewelry stores.

Talking Point

The Princess was made lighter than the typical Model 500 desk phone after the design team at Dreyfuss and Associates noticed teen girls chatting to friends while relaxing on their beds—with the heavy base of the extension on their stomachs.

Little Black Dress Phone

In 1963, Bell introduced several new colors to its Princess line, including black—said to be because first lady Jacqueline Kennedy asked for it. Though black was the standard, default color for other phones, it was by-request-only in Princess models.

Buttoned Down

Bell came out with a push-button Princess in 1963; 12-button models, which included the pound and star keys, came out in 1968. Several other modifications, including message-waiting lights and hold options, were added to the Princess over the years, until AT&T discontinued it in 1994.

America has fallen in love with the new *Princess* phone

in white, beige, pink, blue and turquoise—attractively priced

it's little!... it's lovely!... it lights!

Small size is one reason why the Princess is so popular. It fits where you couldn't have an extension before—on a kitchen counter, a desk or a bedside table.

Graceful styling lets you put the Princess anywhere in your home and be sure that its lovely lines and the color you choose will blend in beautifully.

Lighted dial glows in the dark, brightens for easy dialing when you lift the receiver. Order from our Business Office or ask your telephone man.

BELL TELEPHONE SYSTEM

Early ads for the Princess phone directly targeted women and teen girls. ★

SMART BY DESIGN

If one person could be said to be behind the look of the mid-20th century, it would be Henry Dreyfuss. Born in Brooklyn, NY, in 1904, Dreyfuss went to art school, but after graduating, he pursued industrial design, which was just beginning to take off in the 1920s.

Dreyfuss pioneered what came to be called ergonomics—designing around the human form and behavior—and his clients included industry giants such as New York Central Railroad, Bell, John Deere, Honeywell and Hoover.

Along with the popular Princess phone, his most famous household product designs include:

★ Big Ben alarm clock for Westclox (1939)
★ Model 500 desk phone for Bell (1949)
★ Circular wall thermostat for Honeywell (1953)
★ Constellation vacuum for Hoover (1955)
★ SX-70 camera and case for Polaroid, above (1972)

VIVA FIESTA

THE VIBRANT AMERICAN-MADE POTTERY HAS BRIGHTENED TABLES SINCE THE 1930s.

Designed by Frederick Hurten Rhead for Homer Laughlin China Co. in Newell, West Virginia, Fiesta ware began its iconic history at the Pittsburgh China and Glass Show in 1936. The original colors were red, yellow, cobalt blue, green and ivory; turquoise came along a year later. The genius of the line was in how colors could be mixed and matched; consumers could buy single pieces instead of full sets—a concession to the limited means of the average Depression-era household.

Rhead's art deco design featured concentric circles that made it look as if pieces had been formed by hand on a potter's wheel. In fact, the china was mass-produced and sold at department stores and five-and-dimes like Woolworths. A 24-piece place setting cost about $11 in the 1930s.

Homer Laughlin produced more than 1 million pieces of Fiesta by 1938. The line's popularity grew in part because the company continually brought out new shades to suit changing tastes—soft pastels in the 1950s, brighter hues in the early '60s. Some collectors have a special affection for the old orange-red glaze, sometimes called "radioactive red," produced throughout the early '40s. When a key ingredient in the color formula—uranium—was restricted to government use for nuclear bomb research (the Manhattan Project), red Fiesta disappeared; it returned to shelves in 1959.

After Fiesta's peak in 1948, when 10 million pieces were shipped, demand steadily declined until the line was retired in the early 1970s.

In 1986, Bloomingdale's, the department store chain, partnered with Homer Laughlin to reintroduce the colorful dishware. Modern Fiesta, known as Post 86, is lead-free and safe to use in the microwave and dishwasher.

Although popular with collectors, Fiesta ware also is cherished by families, who pass it down through generations to grace holiday tables each year.

★ Frank McNamara, founder of Diners Club, held the card with the company's first assigned number, 1000. Company lore has it that McNamara's embarrassment over forgetting his wallet was the impetus for the card, but that's actually a PR invention.

CHARGE CARD

DINERS CLUB INTRODUCED a new way to pay in 1950: Charge it. The Diners Club Card, and the many cards it inspired, went hand-in-glove with expense accounts, which multiplied after World War II. Rather than hand it over to the IRS, companies could use their income to entertain clients, and paying for an expensive meal with nothing but a card and a signature gave a businessman cachet. The balance was due at the end of the month, although there was no penalty for late payment—Diners Club made money from the 7% fee it charged merchants.

BY **NATALIE WYSONG**

THAT'S A WRAP

Looking to keep more leftovers around longer, or giving a food gift? These products have it covered.

'54

Take your favorite cheese, for instance . . .

ONLY
SARAN WRAP

will keep it so fresh,
so long . . . so easily!

IT CLINGS BY ITSELF . . . just press it in place, it stays

IT'S MOISTURE-PROOF . . . keeps odors in their place, too

IT'S CRYSTAL-CLEAR . . . you can <u>see</u> everything you wrap

See **MEDIC**   Critics call this the most dramatic television show of the year! See it Monday evenings at 9, EST . . . NBC-TV.

A product of The Dow Chemical Company, Midland, Michigan. Also available in Canada.

'62

you're proud of what you're giving, show it – in sparkling, clear Saran Wrap

What are you cooking up for Christmas? Fruitcakes, candies, your traditional bread recipes, cookies? Give them all a tempting new twist. Present them deliciously on view—gift wrapped in Saran Wrap.* Brilliant idea! Clings better to any shape. Keeps freshness and richness in.

Keeps mouths watering, too. Shows off your gifts like no other wrap. Copy the ideas on this page or create your own with Saran Wrap—give all the gifts from your kitchen even more good taste and originality this Christmas.
A PRODUCT OF THE DOW CHEMICAL COMPANY Dow

Fresh Outlook

Like so many inventions, Saran Wrap started life as a mistake—a sticky, waterproof film that clung to the bottom of lab beakers at Dow in the 1930s. The military sprayed it on planes during WWII, and it was approved for household use in 1953. Saran's edge over Reynolds Wrap was that you could see through it.

Toothsome Test of Freshness!

Here's a double demonstration with a moral. Mom is tasting salad greens tucked away days ago in an "envelope" of Reynolds Wrap...and stored in the refrigerator. How fresh they keep in that pure aluminum foil! And Sis is at her favorite treat...cookies kept crackling crisp in a wonderful gleaming package. Full-flavored, delicious!

Mom and Sis are really demonstrating the same means to supreme freshness...Reynolds Wrap Aluminum Packaging. It's the most advanced protection known to science! All the famous-brand cookies you see here are quality-protected in Reynolds Wrap Aluminum Packaging...as you may have known, from their special sparkle on the market shelves.

Now there's something beyond that gleam of aluminum to guide you in your shopping. On more and more packaged products you'll find the Reynolds Wrap Aluminum Packaging Seal denoting protected quality!

Reynolds Metals Company,
General Sales Office, Louisville 1, Ky.

Nursing...   the career with a future.

QUALITY PROTECTED WITH
REYNOLDS WRAP
ALUMINUM PACKAGING
TRADE MARK

SEE "MISTER PEEPERS,"
Starring Wally Cox,
Sundays NBC-TV Network.

'54

Bright Idea

Originally a maker of cigarette package linings—the founder was related to R.J. Reynolds, the tobacco magnate—Reynolds introduced its aluminum wrap as a general consumer product in 1947. Reynolds Wrap is now regarded as an icon of American culture. A package from the 1950s is housed at the Smithsonian.

PICTURES FROM THE PAST
★ ★ ★ Consumer Demand ★ ★ ★

EARLY ZAPPER

A model flips channels using Zenith's ultrasonic TV remote at a show in 1955. It was a step up from the company's (and the world's) first remote in 1950, the Lazy Bone, which attached to the TV via a long cord; buyers complained that they kept tripping on it.

A LEG UP

A young sailor shops for nylons at Montgomery Ward in New York in 1945. Sales of nylon stockings soared when they returned to shelves after the war, leading to riots in some cities. In Pittsburgh, PA, 40,000 people queued up to snag 13,000 pairs.

LUNCH IN SECONDS

Joanne Meese of Mansfield, OH, prepares baby food in a Tappan microwave in 1955. Ten years earlier, a Raytheon engineer made the accidental discovery of microwave cooking when a candy bar in his pocket melted while he was testing magnetrons.

DISC JOCKEY

A competitive Frisbee flyer sits among discs in 1980. Frisbees were an instant hit when Wham-O brought them to market in 1957. The company sold more than 100 million by 1977.

LOGGING IN

A model lifts a log of Styrofoam to show how light it is in this promotional image. Dow Chemical Co. introduced its brand of polystyrene foam to the market in 1943—and gave the world a new word.

Jungle gyms, such as this hexagonal one at Will Rogers Elementary in Lynwood, CA, have always been built on the principle of active learning. ★

JEWELS OF THE PLAYGROUND

OUTDOOR AMUSEMENT FOR KIDS IS MORE THAN IT SEEMS.

The first jungle gym was installed at a Winnetka, Illinois, school more than 100 years ago. It came out of a meeting of the minds between a progressive educator and Sebastian Hinton, a Chicago lawyer.

Hinton grew up playing on a homemade bamboo grid. His mathematician father believed that moving in real 3D space made it easier for kids to understand math.

The shift in the early 1900s toward focusing on the lives of children—and the role of play in growth and learning for them—put jungle gyms at the center of the playground.

BY **NATALIE WYSONG**

Off the Streets

Mid-1800s social reformers were the first to push for separate play areas. Neighborhoods grew crowded, and busy streets and alleys were dangerous for children. Their natural energy was seen as a force to be directed, and so playgrounds were necessary for proper moral development. Designers added a Children's District to plans for New York City's Central Park, where children and their caregivers could enjoy fresh air and boys played ball. An 1895 state law mandated that schools must include a playground.

Child's Play

Winnetka's young superintendent, Carleton Washburne, upset the educational apple cart with his whole-child model in the 1920s. He believed kids advanced fastest when their emotional, social and intellectual needs were considered, and they could express creativity through play. Schools rushed to copy Winnetka's child-centered classrooms and playground, with innovative jungle gym.

Useful Art

By design or necessity, natural materials and simple structures were the '30s and '40s norm for children's play equipment. Modernist playgrounds, promoted by the Museum of Modern Art's playground exhibit in 1954, placed good design at the center of everyday life. Artists such as Joseph Brown introduced art to children's creative play with sculptural pieces. Novelty equipment built to resemble animals and rockets fired imaginations.

Basic equipment over a packed dirt surface, above, keeps girls busy at an Irwinville, GA, school in 1938; National Merry-Go-Round Day started in 2014 to celebrate the U.S. patent issued in 1871 to William Schneider of Davenport, IA, the first for that classic playground ride.

Brain Games

Charles Hinton built a 3D frame out of bamboo to teach his children geometry. He called out coordinates on the grid and his children scrambled to get to the point first. In a meeting with educator Carleton Washburne, Hinton's son Sebastian later described the fun of climbing on the structure, which led to their work together designing the prototype jungle gym.

No Running on the Playground

The thrill of a towering slide or sky-high monkey bars was in the peril it presented. In 1972, Congress formed the Consumer Product Safety Commission, which began to track emergency room visits and found that many injuries to kids happened at playgrounds.

Equipment got curvier and lower to the ground, and sharp and splintery edges gave way to smooth painted metal. Wood chips, sand or rubber mulch replaced asphalt and packed dirt. But kids being kids, they changed the challenge, flying off swings and jumping from slides, counting on a soft landing.

The old welded steel cubes have become relics, but kids' tendency to push the limit ensures there's no such thing as a playground that's perfectly safe.

Modern jungle gym designs softened angular cubes into friendlier structures. Children flock to this dome at the New York City Housing Authority's Alfred E. Smith Houses on the Lower East Side in 1956. ★

To Frank.
many thanks

ZAMBONI'S SMOOTH MOVE

FROM CALIFORNIA, HYPNOTIC ICE RESURFACER STILL A COOL STAR.

A n inveterate tinkerer, Frank Zamboni set himself the task of finding a better way to clear the ice at his family-run rink in sunny Southern California. Frank and his brother Lawrence opened Iceland skating rink in 1940 in Paramount, south of Los Angeles, and it was a hit. But skaters' enthusiasm waned when they had to wait for the ice resurfacing—an arduous process that involved pulling a scraper behind a tractor, scooping up the scrapings, squeegeeing the dirty water, then spraying the cleared surface with more water.

Zamboni tinkered for seven years until in 1949 he had Model A, made of Army surplus, including jeep parts. With its exposed workings, it resembled a Rube Goldberg contraption, but it reduced ice resurfacing from over an hour to several minutes.

Today's machines are boxy-sleek and as much a crowd-pleaser at hockey games as the main event. As Charles Schulz's alter ego Charlie Brown said: "There are three things in life that people like to stare at—a flowing stream, a crackling fire and a Zamboni clearing the ice."

BY **MARY-LIZ SHAW**

1950

Norwegian skating sensation Sonja Henie is at the Paramount rink when she sees the Model A and has to have one—two, actually. Frank Zamboni builds the first on a tight turnaround to have it ready for her skating show in Chicago. The iceman puts the parts in a U-Haul, hitches it to the jeep that will be the base, and drives it to Illinois. Henie's Model Bs are two of only four made. Zamboni founds company that same year.

1953

The U.S. Patent Office grants Frank Zamboni's application for an Ice Rink Resurfacing Machine. But Zamboni has never stopped modifying his creation and is already on Model D when his patent comes through. By the end of 1954, the company has produced a total of 17 resurfacers.

1954

The Boston Bruins are the first NHL team to use a Zamboni resurfacer. The Boston Garden's Model E21 becomes a star in its own right and now lives in the Hockey Hall of Fame.

1960

Zamboni provides six machines for the Winter Olympics in Squaw Valley, California. Two of the machines are electric-powered.

1967

To meet demand in a hockey-crazed country, Zamboni opens a Canadian branch about an hour west of Toronto, in Brantford, Ontario. The same year, in the same city, 6-year-old Wayne Gretzky is already playing hockey with much older boys—and scoring his way to future fame.

1970

Adapting principles used to create his ice resurfacers, Zamboni devises a water-clearing machine for AstroTurf-covered stadiums. The machine sucks up about 400 gallons a minute.

1980

Charles Schulz first mentions Zamboni machines in his *Peanuts* comic strip. In December of that year, he shows Snoopy driving one. Schulz was an avid hockey fan and player, and used Zamboni resurfacers for his home rink in Minnesota.

1990

The Zamboni Co. introduces Model 552, which will become its most popular electric-powered ice resurfacer.

2006

Two parks department employees of Ice World in Boise, Idaho, take a pair of Zamboni machines, valued at $75,000 each, on a midnight joy ride to the Burger King drive-thru. Parks manager Jim Hall tells the *Boise Guardian* the stunt is "one of the five stupidest things I have seen in 35 years of parks work." Hall fires the men and muses about having them charged with operating unlicensed vehicles on a public street. Given that the machines don't go over 10 mph, "there is little chance of a speeding conviction," the *Guardian* editors conclude.

Model A was only used at Paramount Iceland skating rink, which is still operating. The restored Model A is now on display there. ★

IBM took five years to build the Harvard Mark I, which was in use from 1944 to 1959. Sections of the machine now reside at the Smithsonian. ★

MATH'S BEST FRIEND

THE GREATEST ADVANCE IN ARITHMETIC.

F rom behemoths that took up entire rooms to free virtual varieties found on smartphones, calculators have come a long way since 1944, when Harvard University took delivery of a giant computing machine that came to be known as the Mark I. Invented by grad student Howard Aiken in 1937, Mark I was built by IBM and assembled at Harvard

for use by the military. From that auspicious start, the calculator has become a tool most of us couldn't do without. It has played a pivotal role in science, industry and every field ruled by numbers. In its honor, here's a digit-happy look at how far the calculator has come through the years.

BY **RACHAEL LISKA**

750,000

The number of parts in IBM's Automatic Sequence Controlled Calculator (Mark I), the largest electromechanical calculator at the time (1944). At 5 tons, 51 feet long and 8 feet high, it's the first operational machine that executes long computations automatically.

1

The time in seconds it takes the Harvard Mark I to complete a random multiplication calculation.

A crack team handled Mark I under Navy Cmdr. Howard Aiken (seated center), including Lt. Grace Hopper, one of four original coders.

1967

Texas Instruments invents the first electronic hand-held calculator.

12

The number of digits displayed in red on the first pocket-size calculator to use an LED display. Officially named the Busicom LE-120A, it's casually known as the "HANDY" and retails for $395 in 1971.

$149.95

The suggested retail price for the TI-2500 DataMath calculator when it arrives on the market in April 1972.

1974

Hewlett-Packard develops a compact programmable calculator: HP-65. It is designed to assist in repeated calculations, and it proves useful in engineering, finance, statistics, aviation and general science fields.

$24.95

Price for the Japanese-made Teal LC811, a calculator featuring a liquid crystal display, in 1977.

TI-1766

Model number of Texas Instruments' first solar-powered calculator, introduced in 1981.

1993

Apple releases the Newton PDA (personal digital assistant) featuring a virtual digital calculator. Over the next 10 or so years, virtual calculators become standard on mobile devices like the BlackBerry and iPhone, spelling the end of the independent calculator.

422

Bytes of memory available in the Casio fx-7000G, the first graphing calculator. It can run 10 programs and offers 82 scientific functions.

15

The number of seconds it takes Scott Flansburg of Phoenix, Arizona, to add a randomly selected two-digit number (38) to itself 36 times without using a calculator, winning the Guinness World Records title of Fastest Human Calculator in 2000.

2010

Casio debuts PRIZM, which allows students to create graphs on full-color images.

Programmer Grace Hopper coined the term "computer bug" after finding a moth stuck inside Harvard's Mark II computer in 1947. ★

YOU'RE WEARING THAT?

FASHION HAS ALWAYS MOVED FASTER THAN PUBLIC OPINION.

BY **NATALIE WYSONG**

A notice banning Bermuda shorts causes consternation among male students at Los Angeles City College in 1958. ★

WARDROBE INJUNCTION

Bermuda shorts, hot pants, jeans, nylons, pants (for girls, at least)—all these styles at one time or another exposed wearers to the attention of the fashion police, if not the real police. Here's a look back at when things got the eye.

Modesty Proposal

Depending on one's sex, showing leg was either informal or immoral. Up to midcentury, the suit was a man's go-to outfit, from the office to a baseball game. Too-casual clothing, unless work related, was bad form; shorts, most informal of all, were for sport. But patrolling propriety was a lost cause: At Dartmouth College in 1930, 600 male students protested to wear their "delegged" trousers.

Women faced worse judgment. Even at beaches, police checked hemlines to ensure legs were legal. As late as 1952, the City Council in Fort Worth, Texas, made national news when it considered a shorts ban, after a complaint they were "an advertisement for adultery." The city chose not to pass any "leg"-islation.

Seen It All

With an inseam of only a few inches, hot pants were a '30s design meant for beach- and sports-wear, but fashionistas in the '70s dared to wear the super short, racy pants to the disco and in public.

Nylon Hits a Snag

When DuPont's resilient synthetic fabric in the form of stockings went on sale in 1940, it was a sensation. Replacing delicate silk and rayon, the new style of hosiery sold out quickly. Shorter hemlines showed more leg, and nylon hosiery became a wardrobe must-have.

Or so women thought. The miracle fabric also turned out to be ideal for parachutes, netting and fuel tanks, and as the U.S. economy turned to war production, style stepped aside. What were beautiful legs in comparison to the needs of the defense effort?

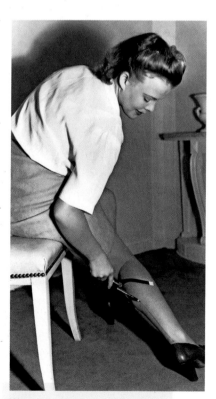

Women give up nylons and resort to leg makeup, for our boys. ★

American Icon

Durable, riveted trousers made by Jacob Davis and Levi Strauss caught on with gold rush miners in the West and with farm workers everywhere.

In the '50s, movie stars Marlon Brando and James Dean established the pants as the uniform of the rebel, and schools rushed to ban them.

In the '60s, protesters made jeans a symbol of activist youth. As the American classic went international, all hopes of banning jeans faded.

The Way of the Bustle

Mary Tyler Moore's emphasis on showing a '60s TV character who did her everyday chores in capris instead of a full skirt put sponsors on edge. But viewers identified with the choice of pants, and the look of women on TV changed for good.

Wearing Pants in the House (and the Senate)

In 1969, U.S. Rep. Charlotte T. Reid, R-Illinois, caused a stir in the House when she wore a black wool pantsuit to work. Male members scurried to see what the future looked like.

It was another 24 years before U.S. Sen. Carol Moseley Braun, D-Illinois, bucked tradition in the Senate.

Tight Pants Strike

Pat Morris was dismissed from her shift at an Oregon plywood mill in 1966 for wearing pants that were distractingly tight. Morris argued that she was dressed like the other employees, and her co-workers went on strike in support. After a week, an agreement was reached for Morris to return to work. She did, wearing baggy pants.

PICTURES FROM THE PAST
★★★ Suited for Leisure ★★★

POWDER BLUE
I wanted to give my husband, Warren, something special for his 35th birthday in 1975. I made him this leisure suit. It was pretty bright, but he wore it proudly.

MARILYN MOHRHUSEN
MORGAN HILL, CA

MORE TO COME!
In 1974 I talked my husband, Joe, into entering a fashion show wearing the leisure suit I made for him. He took first prize—$15. I used his winnings to buy more polyester knit.

ANITA ALCORN OAK RIDGE, TN

STYLE TIMES TWO

This navy blue suit was one of two in my closet in 1976. The other was a nice forest green with the same stitching and shoulder epaulets.

RANDALL STOUGH OTTAWA, OH

WASH, WEAR, REPEAT

I loved the leisure suits of the 1970s because not only could you toss them in the washer and dryer, it was impossible to wrinkle the fabric. Come Sunday, my boys Dan (left) and Dave would be complaining before I opened their closet. They said the suits were too itchy, too tight or too hot. Too bad! Little do they know, I've kept one of the suits—in case I ever have a grandson. Their sister Jennifer escaped leisure-suit torture.

JUDY SIKORSKI ROSSFORD, OH

FOR DRESSING UP

Here I am in the only leisure suit I ever owned. I wore it to church and special occasions. This picture was taken in 1973 outside our home in Oregon. With me are my wife, Janet, and our children Linda and Eric.

ROBERT KRAHMER
CORVALLIS, OR

OVER HILL, DALE AND EVERYWHERE

THE DRAB GREEN VEHICLE THAT POWERED THROUGH WAR.

G en. George Marshall called it "America's greatest contribution to modern warfare." GIs called it the Jeep, a nickname of obscure origin that may have come from a *Popeye* cartoon or a light tractor Minneapolis-Moline sold to the Army before World War II. The Jeep put the American military and its allies on wheels.

After WWII, the Jeep settled into civilian life and morphed into the first sport utility vehicle, the Wagoneer. But the mission that inspired its creation in 1941—to take you anywhere you want to go—lives on. Today, Jeep is Fiat Chrysler's most popular brand in the U.S., with more than 900,000 sold in 2019.

The original concept came from American Bantam, a manufacturer of small vehicles that occasionally served as props in movies (Donald Duck's cartoon roadster was a Bantam). Its Bantam Reconnaissance Car won the War Department contract, but the plant couldn't meet demand. The government sought more makers to roll out the vehicle in large numbers.

Willys-Overland and Ford were the main Jeep makers in WWII. Ford called its prototype GP. Some speculate the Jeep name is a sounding out of those initials. The two companies produced about 650,000 Willys MBs and Ford GPWs, their respective labels for what were essentially similar vehicles.

Willys trademarked Jeep after the war and hired designer Brooks Stevens to adapt it to civilian use. Stevens, the man behind Oscar Mayer's iconic Wienermobile, created Jeepster and later Wagoneer, which was produced without fundamental changes from 1963 to '91.

Before the Jeepster, Willys was sold in 1953 to industrialist Henry J. Kaiser, who entered the car business after building Liberty ships for the war effort. He dropped production of his unprofitable Henry J and other cars, and concentrated more on marketing Jeeps. Kaiser Jeep was sold to American Motors Corp. in 1970; Chrysler acquired the brand when it absorbed AMC in 1987.

BY **RUSS MAKI**

Despite many brand owners through the years, Jeep keeps on rolling along.

Ray Harroun and his Marmon Wasp buzz past the competition in the first Indianapolis 500. ★

BRICKYARD TRACKS RACING'S PAST

1911 COMPETITION A CHECKERED FIRST LAP FOR BELOVED INDY 500.

One of the jewels in the triple crown of auto racing is the Indianapolis 500. Its venue, the Indianapolis Motor Speedway, was built in 1909 as a test track for Indiana's then-burgeoning automotive industry.

The state's historic automakers—Studebaker, Stutz and Auburn among them—have faded into the past. But the Indy 500 lives on, despite a few interruptions, such as during wartime, and postponements, most recently in 2020, when the COVID-19 pandemic delayed the race until Aug. 23.

The track began with a surface of tar-covered gravel, but once races were staged there, the primitive pavement proved quite dangerous, disintegrating in the turns and spattering drivers with debris. Track co-owner Charles Fisher remedied the problem by paving the track with 3.2 million bricks—thus was born the track's iconic nickname, the Brickyard. While nearly all of the track has been overlaid in asphalt since then, a 36-inch stretch of brickwork at the start/finish line remains exposed in homage to the track's history.

The first Indy 500 winner in 1911 was Ray Harroun in the Wasp built by the Marmon Motor Car Co., yet another Indiana auto manufacturer. Harroun, who was an engineer, added an innovation to his yellow and black racer that has become standard in all motor vehicles: a rearview mirror.

Harroun's win was controversial for two reasons. First, he drove without a mechanic as passenger, then the norm, to monitor oil pressure and act as a spotter. Second, a wreck during the race may have caused scorekeepers to lose count of laps completed by second-place finisher Ralph Mulford—known as the Gumdrop Kid for his love of the candy. Mulford protested the results, but Harroun was declared the winner after a review of the race's limited records. The 500 was the last major race of Harroun's driving career.

BY **RUSS MAKI**

James' used Ford Custom came with all the extras.

CRUISING IN THE FORD

PARENTS PUT THE BRAKES ON BORROWING THE FAMILY CAR.

One Sunday the girl I was dating—her name escapes me—invited me to her house in Lincoln Park, Michigan. At 17, I had my temporary license and had already suffered the humiliation of Dad driving us to a school dance. Now he was asleep in front of the TV, and the car keys were in their usual spot in the kitchen. As I drove from Allen Park to her house, I put on the latest Detroit doo-wop so I'd look cool as I drove up.

We cruised down Fort Street and went to the drive-in for a malt and skinny fries before I got nervous. At home, I faced the firing squad. My Lincoln Park sweetie didn't wait for me while I was grounded for four weeks, and she moved on to date someone who had a car.

I'd saved $500, and Mom thought it was time Dad used his influence as a Ford employee to get me the best deal on a used car. That shopping day was one of the most important of my young life. We found a 1951 powder blue Ford Custom with baby

> WE FOUND A 1951 POWDER BLUE FORD CUSTOM WITH BABY MOON HUBCAPS AND BUBBLE SKIRTS.
> ★

moon hubcaps and bubble skirts. It even had air conditioning and a radio. After much dialogue, Dad and the salesman agreed on $800, with Dad putting in the extra for me.

Two weeks later, it was my turn to drive my friends on a Friday night. Joe, Norm and I headed for Michigan Avenue in Dearborn, which was jammed with custom hot rods. With windows down and moving at a crawl, we tried our best to get the attention of the cute girls at the drive-ins. I wasn't watching traffic in front of me, and with a loud thud I hit the rear of a black 1950 Ford. There was no damage to the older couple's car, but my front end was smashed. They felt sorry for me and, luckily, the only expense was replacing my custom Pontiac grill.

Dad thought it was a lesson learned, and all Mom could do was laugh. From then on, I kept my eyes on the road, no matter how cute the girls were.

JAMES FARKAS NORTHVILLE, MI

A DREAM OF A CAR

THE VIEW WAS SUPERB—UNTIL THE SUN CAME OUT.

Before I bought this rare car, one like it appeared in my dreams, being lifted by a yard crew to be dropped into a crusher. I sprinted toward it, waving my arms and screaming "Stop!" Since getting a 1956 Ford Fairlane Crown Victoria Skyliner coupe two years ago, nights are more restful.

The transparent roof offers some benefits of a convertible. However, even with tinted glass and a zip-in fabric liner, the cabin overheats in the sun. This oversight hurt sales. In 1954, when the roof option was first offered, 13,000 were sold; by the end of its three-year run, only 602 sold.

This car has nearly every option available for the model year: a 312-cubic-inch V-8, power steering

> ## I DON'T MIND ROLLING THE WINDOWS DOWN, BUT I WISH IT HAD AIR CONDITIONING.
> ★

and seat, dual spotlights, continental kit, wire wheel covers and Town and Country radio. Oddly, with all the power accessories, it has manual crank windows. I don't mind rolling the windows down, but I wish it had air conditioning, a pricey option when this car was new.

Many people have never seen a car like this. At one cruise night, a fellow hobbyist swore that I had cut open the roof and installed the transparent panel myself. As he sat in the car, he observed some hairline cracks in the panel. I said, "When you get to be over 60 years old, you'll probably have a few cracks, too."

JOHN H. WALKER PLEASANT HILL, OH

In 1956, a stainless steel tiara on the roof gave the Ford Fairlane Crown Victoria Skyliner its name. ★

The 1969 Chevelle COPO, a limited-edition, used the L72 engine for performance.

BEAUTY AND BEAST

THE CAR CALLED PRINCESS RULED THE STREETS.

For so many people of my generation, the late 1960s was a time of extremes: Woodstock, Vietnam, the moon landing. Even cars were extreme. Half a year's pay would buy a high-performance Mustang fastback, a Pontiac GTO or a Dodge Super Bee.

I was working as an apprentice pipe fitter for Goodyear in Akron when I heard about some limited-production muscle cars at a nearby dealership. They were said to be equipped with 427-cubic-inch engines rated at 425 horsepower. Less than an hour after arriving at the dealership, I bought one, a 1969 Chevelle COPO.

I made a few improvements to what was already one of the fiercest street-legal cars ever produced. Then it was time to race.

There was a lot of street racing in Akron back then. Friday and Saturday nights saw the parking lots of area drive-ins filled with muscle cars. Drivers were just waiting for the next worthy challenge.

> FRIDAY AND SATURDAY NIGHTS SAW THE PARKING LOTS OF AREA DRIVE-INS FILLED WITH MUSCLE CARS.
>
> ★

My car was never beaten while I owned it. But soon after my son was born in the spring of 1970, I sold it. For several decades after that I wondered what had become of the car. Only a few hundred had ever been manufactured.

Then in May 2015 I heard from Phil Wojnarowski, and I almost dropped the phone when he told me he was in possession of the coolest car I'd ever owned. What's more, he was only about 40 miles away! A few days later I made the short trip to see and drive my old racer. Amazingly, it was still in excellent condition. It had the original engine and almost all of its original paint—despite having survived several owners and many runs down quarter-mile drag strips.

Phil and I have since become good friends, sharing our back-in-the-day stories as well as those about the car we like to call Princess. She's in excellent hands now.

JIM WALKER MASSILLON, OH

★★ TRICK RIDE ★★

Here I am at 19 in 1968, with my first car, a '63 Chevy Nova Super Sport.
It had a quirk that made it possible to remove the ignition key while
the car was running. I had fun freaking out all my friends as we barreled
down the highway, asking them to get something out of my locked
glove box—and casually removing the key and handing it over.

MARIE FISHER NASHUA, NH

TASTE OF AMERICANA

Hungry? Join us at the table for a look at how Americans filled their plates in days gone by, and what we still enjoy eating today.

The Track, far left, was an innovation for in-car dining, as at this California drive-in in 1948: Customers parked next to the box and placed their order. The box slid along the track into the restaurant, where it was filled with food and sent back to the customer. Boys eat hot dogs at the state fair in Minnesota, left; and diners gather at a drugstore lunch counter in Washington, D.C., in 1961.

The test kitchen at Campbell's in the '50s was stocked with fixings for invention. ★

SIDE FOR ALL SEASONS

GREEN BEAN CASSEROLE, A HOLIDAY TABLE STAPLE.

Back in 1955, Dorcas Reilly was a supervisor in the test kitchens of Campbell Soup Co. when the Associated Press called with a recipe challenge: Create easy, quick-to-make dishes out of ingredients commonly found in most kitchens. In the mid-1950s, those ingredients probably included cream of mushroom soup and green beans.

Among the many dishes her team came up with for the challenge was a simple casserole Reilly called "Green Bean Bake."

Reilly couldn't have predicted it then, but her side dish was destined to outlive any other recipe she devised in her long career at Campbell's and earn her a place in the National Inventors Hall of Fame.

Today, many Americans don't consider Thanksgiving complete without a green bean casserole on the table next to the bird. Over the years, home cooks tweaked the recipe to make it their own—adding bacon, corn or ham, for instance—but the original is as likely to be the star side on turkey day as any variation.

Though tastes have shifted markedly since the convenience cooking that was the hallmark of midcentury kitchens, people still leave room for Reilly's little side that could. As culinary historian Laura Shapiro told *The New York Times* in 2018, "You will think of it as the food of your past and you will cherish it."

BY **MARY-LIZ SHAW**

6

The number of ingredients in the first test recipe: mushroom soup, green beans, celery salt, soy sauce, french-fried onions and water, according to Dorcas Reilly's original recipe card, below. After tastings, testers used pepper instead of celery salt, and milk later replaced water.

¼ Cup

The amount of french-fried onions added to the sauce after the first experiment. Food historian Laura Shapiro told NPR the casserole's french-fried onions are "the reason people like it decade after decade." Reilly clearly had an instinct for how special they were, for despite complaints from her team about "too many onions," she upped the amount to ⅓ cup, with the rest scattered on top. The modern recipe calls for stirring in ⅔ cup onions.

4

Variations of the green bean bake Campbell's tested between April 11 and May 17, 1955, as recorded on the recipe card. After one taste test, Reilly noted that the casserole "needs more pep" and stirred in some extra soy sauce. Several more tests were recorded on the card between '58 and '63.

20 Million

The estimated number of households that serve green bean casserole on Thanksgiving every year, according to Campbell's.

It's a side dish with a festive side.

CAMPBELL'S GREEN BEAN CASSEROLE
Prep Time: 10 min. Bake Time: 30 min.

Come Home To A Home-Cooked Meal.

1960

The year Campbell's first put the recipe for Green Bean Casserole on cream of mushroom soup labels.

10,000

The average number of requests to Campbell's each year for its green bean casserole recipe.

40

The approximate annual percentage of Campbell's cream of mushroom soup sales that are used to make green bean casserole.

92

Dorcas Reilly's age at her death in October 2018.

2002

The year Campbell's donated Reilly's Green Bean Bake recipe card to the National Inventors Hall of Fame.

Dorcas Reilly, below, didn't know her green bean dish was so popular until years after she invented it. She retired from Campbell's in 1988.

VEGETABLE - OVEN

MUSHROOM - Green Bean - French Fried Onion

Ingredients	EXP I 4/13/55 JP	EXP II 4/19/55 JP	EXP III 5/17/55 JP	EXP IV 5/17/55	EXP V 6/10/58 JP	EXP VI 6/10/58 JM	EXP VII 6/12/58 BC	EXP VIII 4/1/59 MG	EXP IX 10/19/60 BC
Source			3/4/58						TM
Source			JP						10/20/60
Temp./Time									
Yield									
drained - beans french style green	2 boxes	2 boxes	2 boxes	2 boxes	-----	-----	-----	-----	-----
Water	3/4 cup	/	-----	-----	-----	---	-----	-----	
Mushroom soup	1 can	1 can	1 can	1 can	1 can	1 can	1 can	1 can	1 can
Celery salt	1/4 tsp	-----	-----	-----	-----	-----	-----	-----	
Soy sauce	1/4 t.	1/3 t. & 1/2 t.	1 tsp.	-----	1 tsp.	1 tsp.	1 tsp.	1 tsp.	1 tsp.
Pepper		freshly ground	/	/	Dash	Dash	Dash	Dash	Dash
French fried onion	3½oz. 1 can	3½ oz. 1 can	3½oz. 1 can	frozen pkg.	3½ oz. 1 can	3½oz. 1 can	3½oz. 1 can	1 can	1 can
...rshire	-----	/	-----	1/2 tsp.					
...rained	-----	-----	-----	-----	canned 3 cups	cooked 2-1/8 (canned)	french fried 2 cans (3 cups)	frozen 2 pkg.	frozen 2 pkg.
						1 can			
...d								6 slices	
			OK						OK

- Cook green beans in water. Meanwhile blend soup with 1/3 cup cooking water, celery, salt, soy sauce and pepper in a 1 1/2 quart casserole. Mix in cooked beans. Top with onions. Bake at 350 for 20 to 30 minutes. TASTED BY: EH, JM, JR, DF, JP - all liked - lost flavor of soy and celery salt. EH would like onions in basic recipe.
EXP II - Made the same way as before - TASTED BY: JM, JR, JP. I put 1/4 cup of onion in sauce and baked for 20 mi n. at 350. Too brown on top. Needs more pep, so stirred in extra soy sauce -

99-X-6152

RECIPE TWEAK YIELDS DISAPPOINTING RESULTS

AT HOLIDAY MEALS, my mom cooked different meats—ham at Easter, turkey at Thanksgiving, spaghetti with breaded chicken at Christmas—but she served the same sides every time. Her version of the green bean casserole featured golden corn soup and slivered almonds.

When I got married, I decided my contribution to Thanksgiving dinner that year would be green bean casserole. I baked it in my new, modern-looking Pyrex dish.

At dinner, I arrogantly placed the casserole in the center of the table and eagerly waited for everyone to try it and tell me how wonderful it was.

But as my family ate it, the comments were not quite what I was expecting. They said it didn't taste the same as Mom's.

The problem was I'd used cream of broccoli soup instead of golden corn soup. We all had a good laugh, and despite my misstep, I was assigned to bring the casserole every holiday.

Pam loved to cook with her mom, Eleanor Dvorsak. ★

Over the years, whether my casserole was good or bad, I loved sharing the kitchen with my mom and learning all the family secrets. Our time together was priceless; I'll always cherish it.

PAM TABONE SLOVAN, PA

FRENCH-FRIED TO A CRISP

One year our family was at Mom's for Thanksgiving and oven space was in short supply. My sister-in-law Shelly, who is an excellent cook, put the green bean casserole under the broiler to cook it faster. But within minutes, the french-fried onions had caught fire! We rushed the casserole to the garage, put out the flames and with a few touch-ups, were able to bring it to the table. Now, no Thanksgiving is complete without someone saying, "Remember when Shelly tried to burn the house down?" In this picture, Shelly is fourth from left, and I'm fifth from left with my arm around Mom.

DIANE JOCKISCH SHERMAN, IL

That dish in front may well be a green bean casserole, says Joan, at rear right. ★

FROM TEST KITCHEN TO SOUP LABEL

FORMER CAMPBELL'S EMPLOYEE RECALLS HOW RECIPES MADE IT TO THE MENU.

W hen the green bean casserole recipe was developed in 1955, I worked for Campbell's as the secretary to the publicity manager in the home economics department, which is where all the recipes for the company's products were developed, tested and finalized.

One of the perks of working in that department was getting to taste-test recipes before they were presented to the marketing and advertising managers. It's very possible that I taste-tested the green bean casserole, but it was so long ago that I can't be sure. I can say that many excellent recipes were developed in the test kitchens, and I enjoyed tasting many of them.

I worked often with Dorcas Reilly, test kitchen supervisor and the inventor of the

> I WORKED OFTEN WITH DORCAS REILLY, TEST KITCHEN SUPERVISOR AND THE INVENTOR OF THE GREEN BEAN CASSEROLE.
>
> ★

green bean casserole. Dorcas' group developed the recipes, and we publicized them and the products that were used as the ingredients. We sent newsletters to food editors in radio, TV, newspapers and magazines once a month, and we featured new recipes, with suggestions for how to prepare and serve them.

Several years after Dorcas and I left Campbell's to raise our children, Dorcas started doing freelance work. She contacted me, and invited me to join her in producing a cookbook for a client. We worked together for about six years, producing cookbooks, recipe folders and mailings. Dorcas was a very talented lady.

JOAN KNISELL PENNSAUKEN, NJ

PICTURES FROM THE PAST
★ ★ ★ Quick Service ★ ★ ★

FAST FOOD ROYALTY
Originally Insta-Burger King, the chain's first restaurant opened in Miami, FL, in 1954. The Whopper was born three years later and soon was touted on signs, as on this drive-in around 1960.

ON THE RUN ⌃
Customers shop at an early drive-through grocery in Los Angeles in 1949. The term, later shortened to drive-thru, was added to Merriam-Webster's that year.

A SIP OF HISTORY «
Shoppers look over the menu outside the first Starbucks in Seattle's Pike Place Market. The cafe that set off a retailing juggernaut opened in 1971.

SIDES BY SIDE ON TURKEY DAY

Foods next to the bird fill in the picture nicely.

Green Bean Vinaigrette

Campbell's made green bean casserole, with mushroom soup and french-fried onions, a must-have side at Thanksgiving when it created the recipe in 1955. But green beans were at festive tables long before, as this Stokely's ad proves.

Dip It Good!

The combo of dry onion soup mix and sour cream was first called California Dip in 1954, after a Golden State home cook whipped it up. Lipton's soup mix, introduced in 1952, and ridged potato chips (about 1948) form a perfect example of midcentury convenience— the starter you make in minutes and eat simply with your fingers.

The Golden Arches migrated to the McDonald's logo in 1962. ★

FROM DINER TO McDONALD'S

EACH EATERY OFFERS A BUFFET OF MEMORIES.

After posting a request on Facebook for a photo of the Cottage Diner, my favorite place to eat growing up in Monongahela in the 1970s, I was flooded with stories. One person shared a hilarious tale from his early teens when, during a sleepover, he and his friends crept into the alley behind the diner at 4 a.m. and stole pies out of the back of the delivery truck.

Many remembered having a sandwich at the diner after a movie at the Star Theater just around the corner. Nearby Frank's Fruit Market sold beautiful wrapped fruit baskets and Christmas trees in the open plaza. A taxi stand and a Greyhound stop next door meant you could grab a snack at the diner while waiting for the bus. The memories go back to the '50s, when my mom went there.

During redevelopment in the '80s, the entire block was wiped out. A shiny McDonald's now stands in place of the diner. Its owner has become a generous community member. My children and I hit the drive-thru whenever we crave a Big Mac and a sweet thick shake.

But so many images of the old diner stay with me. I share them with my children, but they can't know the pleasure we took in the not-so-perfect architecture, the not-so-comfortable wooden booths, the not-so-healthy fries cooked in pots of well-used grease or the not-so-pleasant whiff of ripe produce through the open diner window on a warm summer day.

SHERRI VIZZUETT MONONGAHELA, PA

★ ★ ★

"TWO ALL-BEEF PATTIES, SPECIAL SAUCE..."

After Pittsburgh, PA, owner/operator Jim Delligatti formulated what would become its signature sandwich in 1967, McDonald's introduced the Big Mac to all franchisees in 1968.

The Name
Esther Rose, 21, a secretary at an advertising agency in 1967, pitched the name Big Mac—thus officially labeling the now-famous sandwich.

The Price
After launching in 1968 for 49 cents, a Big Mac today is $4 to $5 or more.

The Index
Devised by *The Economist* in 1986, the Big Mac Index is used to compare purchasing power around the globe.

The Museum
In 2007, Delligatti and his family opened a Big Mac Museum Restaurant in North Huntingdon, PA.

The Sales
McDonald's sells more than 550 million Big Macs a year.

The Sauce
Bottles of limited-edition Big Mac sauce priced as high as $10,000 appeared on eBay after McDonald's gave away 10,000 bottles of the tasty condiment in January 2017.

FROZEN IN TIME: TV DINNERS

FRANTIC ATTEMPT TO SAVE TONS OF TURKEY LEADS TO THE LAUNCH OF FROZEN MEALS.

here is some dispute about who originated the very first frozen dinner, but there is no doubt that executives at C.A. Swanson & Sons catapulted the concept into consumer kitchens. An oft-repeated story says the company turned a fowl situation—an excess of Thanksgiving turkey—into a marketing success. The team filled an aluminum tray with turkey supper fixings and dubbed the frozen meal a "TV Dinner." It was easy to reheat and eat in front of the newfangled television sets that were fast becoming centerpieces of American living rooms. Even the packaging of the meals looked like a TV, complete with images of a viewing screen and control knobs. By the end of 1954, millions of Swanson TV Dinners had been sold.

BY **JEANNE AMBROSE**

SUPPER BECOMES TRAY CHIC

TV dinners took off when Swanson marketed them to busy women in the workforce for the first time. "I'm late—but dinner won't be," touted one ad. The history of TV dinners is full of similar milestones.

1930
Clarence Birdseye launches the first line of frozen foods under the label Birds Eye Frosted Food Co. after learning about flash freezing from Inuit fishermen while living in Labrador in Canada.

1940s
Jack Fisher creates FridgiDinners for use as convenient meals in U.S. taverns.

1945
Extra vegetables from his victory garden inspire W.L. Maxson to create Strato-Plates, one of the first complete frozen meals, designed for reheating and serving on military and civilian airplanes.

1949
The first frozen entrees for the home market sell as One-Eyed Eskimo meals by Frozen Dinners Inc. in the Pittsburgh, PA, area. A few years later, the company becomes Quaker State Food Corp., selling 2.5 million entrees by 1954.

1953
Betty Cronin, working for Swanson as a bacteriologist, figures out how the meat, potatoes and vegetables could be heated at one temperature for the same amount of time.

1954
Frozen meals take off big-time when Swanson dubs them "TV Dinners." Sales hit 25 million by year's end.

1960
Swanson TV Dinner trays gain a fourth compartment to accommodate dessert.

1962
Swanson drops the name "TV Dinners" because the meals could be eaten for lunch, too. Or even for breakfast.

1986
The popularity of microwaves prompts Swanson to switch from aluminum to plastic trays.

Clarence Birdseye took a tip from Inuit fishermen about flash freezing.

PICNIC PICKS

For those salad days of summer.

Plain Favorite

First served on hot dogs in 1904 at the St. Louis World's Fair, French's was a standby both at ballparks and on picnic tables. Recipes devised at the Rochester, NY, headquarters at 1 Mustard St. appeared on jar labels and in free leaflets, as this ad offers.

Crafty Tomatoes

The unusual salads here include Two-Way Tempter (far left) with jellied consomme and Miracle Whip, and Sea Isle (center) with shrimp and Kraft Sandwich Spread. French, Miracle French and Casino French dressings might best be called mild, medium and wild, depending on how much garlic you like.

Here's a summer supper you "cook-up" in your refrigerator!

Chilled Treet and Apricot Molds!

Take it easy—let your refrigerator fix supper—a Treet-and-salad supper! Well-chilled Treet tastes so good—it's that flavorful Armour blend of tender pork and sugar-cured ham! And Armour's exclusive middle-of-the-tin opener brings the chilled loaf of Treet out whole—easy to slice evenly. There's no bone or waste—you eat every bite.

Marie Gifford, the famous Armour home economist, suggests serving Treet with molded salads. Stud whole cooked apricots with cloves, set in lemon-flavored gelatin and chill. This refreshing supper is only one of hundreds of easy Armour Pantry-Shelf Meals—but it's one of the most delicious!

Tune in STARS OVER HOLLYWOOD.
On Radio—CBS—Saturday daytime. On Television—NBC—See newspaper for time.

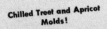

How many good-and-quick Armour Pantry-Shelf Meals from the famous Armour Kitchens do you have on *your* pantry shelf? There are more than 25 different ones—and more than 25 *dozen* different ways to serve them deliciously. Won't you try several—soon?

ARMOUR Pantry-Shelf Meals

Meet Your Treat

Armour Treet was introduced in 1939, two years after Spam, but never was able to overtake its canned competitor. When compared to Spam, Treet is smoother, closer to Vienna sausage, and sweeter, which may explain its being served here with chilled apricot molds. Or maybe not.

SLICES OF WONDER

A SALUTE TO THE LOAF THAT WENT TO PIECES.

R ight from the get-go, Wonder Bread's success was a result of technology and clever marketing—the twin pillars of economic advancement in the first half of the 20th century.

The loaf that came to be called Wonder Bread was developed by the Taggart Baking Co. of Indianapolis, Indiana. An early pioneer in automated baking, Taggart built a factory that was considered state-of-the-art in 1920. It launched Wonder Bread in 1921 after running a series of print ads that talked intriguingly about "wonder" as something to wonder about. There was no mention of bread, but the unique campaign built mystique for a loaf unlike any other on the market.

When it reached stores in May 1921, each loaf of Wonder Bread was 1½ pounds, half again as large as other loaves. And with its soft, springy texture, even crumb and bright color, it neither looked nor tasted like the crusty, rustic loaves made at home. Wonder Bread was a marvel of industrial efficiency, a beacon of the modern age.

Continental Baking Co. bought Taggart in 1925 and sold Wonder Bread across the country. In 1930, Continental introduced sliced Wonder Bread.

Within a few short years, Wonder Bread was on a roll to becoming a lunchbox staple for generations of school kids.

BY **MARY-LIZ SHAW**

Wonder Uncut

In 1943, in the midst of a steel shortage, the government banned sliced bread, which was produced using large automated steel slicers. The ban was lifted two months later.

Vital Vitamins

With the rise of diseases like beriberi and pellagra, caused by vitamin deficiencies, white bread, produced with flour stripped of nutrients, was criticized as being empty food. Under government pressure, Wonder Bread added vitamins and minerals to its flour and touted its bread as "enriched." In the early 1950s, it advertised that it "builds strong bodies eight ways." By the end of the decade, the claim had grown to 12.

Written in Air

As Taggart was getting ready to launch its new industrially processed loaf, company executive Elmer Cline was trying to dream up a name for it. At the International Balloon Race in Indianapolis, he found the answer when the sight of all those hot air balloons filled him with wonder. In 2001, Wonder Bread got its own hot air balloon.

The Wonder Years

Perhaps the brand's most successful slogan was "Make the most of their Wonder Years," promoting the health benefits of feeding Wonder Bread to kids during the formative years up to age 12. The phrase seeped into the national consciousness. In 1988, writers Neal Marlens and Carol Black borrowed *The Wonder Years* for the title of their hit sitcom about growing up in 1960s suburbia.

Have you seen the Wonder balloon? The company tracks sightings on its social media channels. ★

Best Thing Since You-Know-What

The first to bring sliced bread to America was the Chillicothe Baking Co. in Missouri in 1928. It advertised it as "the greatest forward step in the baking industry since bread was wrapped." Later, Wonder Bread kept up a steady campaign touting the virtues of its pre-sliced loaves. But comedian Red Skelton is believed to be the first to utter the phrase we all know today in a 1952 interview with the *Salisbury Times* in Maryland. Don't worry about television, he told the reporter, "it's the greatest thing since sliced bread."

Back From the Brink

Wonder Bread vanished from shelves in 2012 with the bankruptcy of Hostess. But Flowers Foods of Thomasville, Georgia, bought the venerable brand about a year later and has been slowly returning it to stores.

Make the most of their "Wonder Years"

WONDER BREAD

WONDER
ENRICHED
BREAD

Builds Strong Bodies 8 Ways!

Continental Baking Co., Inc.
Raleigh

Wonder Bread claimed its enriched recipe helped kids grow in ads in 1956 (above) and again in 1968 (right).

The "Wonder Years," one through twelve, are the formative years when you can do the most for your child's growth

During these years your children develop in many ways—actually grow to 90% of their adult height. Every delicious slice of Wonder Bread is carefully enriched with foods for growing bodies and minds. The "Wonder Years" come only once.

Make the most of them. Serve your children nutritious Wonder Bread.

Good Housekeeping

WONDER
ENRICHED BREAD

Helps build strong bodies 12 ways!®

Judi dressed the part of Little Miss Sunbeam in 1954. The look was certainly close.

BECOMING MISS SUNBEAM

BREAD COMPANY'S MASCOT CONTEST SPARKS NATIONWIDE FUN.

Do you remember Sunbeam bread? Where I grew up in La Mesa, California, it was very popular. While my mother usually baked her own bread for our family, sometimes we got a loaf of Sunbeam as a treat.

In 1954, when I was 7, my parents entered me in a Little Miss Sunbeam contest. Back then, the bread company held promotional contests in different areas of the country to find Little Miss Sunbeam look-alikes.

My mother and father must have figured I resembled the sunny-haired, blue-eyed mascot. My mother dressed me in a skirt and blouse with a Peter Pan collar and puffy sleeves—the closest we could get to the dress Little Miss Sunbeam wore. She also pinned my ringlets on top of my head and added a pretty satin bow. As fate would have it, nothing came of my entry, which was probably for the best. I was extremely shy, so I never would've been able to cope with the attention, nor was I as poised, polished or outgoing as a real Little Miss Sunbeam should be.

But when I came across that old photo of myself made-up as Little Miss Sunbeam, I was curious about the character, so I did some quick research online and found several old advertisements. It turns out my parents weren't wrong—there was a resemblance!

> MY MOTHER AND FATHER MUST HAVE FIGURED I RESEMBLED THE SUNNY-HAIRED, BLUE-EYED MASCOT.

JUDI CARROLL ESCONDIDO, CA

★ ★ ★ ICE-COLD SMILES ★ ★ ★

My father owned a grocery store in Logan, Ohio, in 1937.
A Coca-Cola salesman called on him, saw me, and asked if he could
take my picture for the company magazine. I was 5 and he told me
I looked like Shirley Temple. I thought it was pretty cool.

ALICE J. HARVEY SCOTTSDALE, AZ

HOME OF THE BRAVE

Wartime stories include heroes of every kind, instances of sacrifice and moments of relief in victory. Along the way, romances bloom.

Sailors, far left, celebrate after hearing the Japanese government has accepted terms of surrender to end World War II; Army veterans en route to Le Havre, France, on their way home in May 1945; below, Korean veterans arrive in New York in 1953: former POW Cpl. Michael Gianinni embraces his mother; and Maj. Joe Palermo greets his wife.

LOVE, LEFTY

PRICELESS DISCOVERY BRINGS JOY AND SOME SURPRISES TO FAMILY.

Don's cartoon of a soldier wrestling with his sleeping bag is still funny years after he drew it in a letter to his gram. ★

Shortly after our dad passed away in 2011, we came upon a shoebox of letters dated from 1946 to 1948. It sat untouched for decades in an attic.

The box was a treasure-trove of correspondence between our father, Donald Pegler, a 17-year-old soldier in the Army in 1946, and his family in Chicago. While the bulk of the letters were written while he was stationed in Japan, his service in Texas and Washington, as well as the arduous voyage to Asia, were also documented. Apparently his parents and Grandma Pearl saved every letter, photograph and cartoon. The collection depicts the life (and imagination) of a young soldier.

We learn how he coped with ailments from scarlet fever to ringworm, insatiable hunger and extreme weather. He describes being severely injured when he drove a jeep into a wire tied across a street.

It was truly priceless reading about the friendship he forged with a Japanese teenager. He talks about the similarities that he noticed between American and Japanese life.

He also covers maintaining old high school friendships and his experiences with other soldiers. He writes of fellow soldiers' struggles, of his high school girlfriends and of the ruins and beauty in places he visited.

Even the small surprises delighted us. For instance, Dad always insisted that he didn't eat candy, yet his correspondence proves that he was quite a fan of candy and fruitcake while he was in the service.

The letters often feature little cartoons he drew that further explain situations he writes about.

But even more profound than the content itself is the obvious familial connection maintained among the young soldier, his parents and his grandmother, whom he always called "Gram."

In a top drawer of his dresser, we found a sketchbook of his Army experiences. The beginning of his sense of humor, for which he was known as an adult, is there on the pages he composed as a teenager.

We collected his correspondence and sketches into a family book called *Miss You All ... Love Lefty*, which is how he signed many of his letters.

Our dad returned home to marry, raise seven kids and thoroughly enjoy a lifelong career in advertising. In 1962, he joined Foote, Cone & Belding in Chicago, where he used his skills as an illustrator and his sense of humor for one of the agency's most successful campaigns: the Raid bug ads for SC Johnson.

In 2015, the Museum of Broadcast Communications named the Raid bugs as one of advertising's 10 greatest icons.

LAURIE PEGLER MALLIN PARK RIDGE, IL

A sketch by Don on the tricky work of erecting a military tent, above; and Fred Pegler carries his son's duffel bag on the day Don left for the Army in 1946.

At 18, Ed Long was a Navy radioman who saw action in the Pacific. ★

TO SERVE AND PROTECT

Our dear friend Ed Long joined the Navy in September 1944 to serve his country and to see the world. After basic training, he spent 20 weeks at the University of Wisconsin-Madison for radio training, where he won an award for copying 1,000 characters of code without error.

While at Leyte in the Philippines, Ed served on the USS *Melvin R. Nawman*. For seven months, the destroyer hunted Japanese subs and protected the USS *Anzio* escort carrier while its planes went on bombing missions.

On Christmas 1945, Ed was assigned to the destroyer USS *Sloat* off Okinawa, where he served until his discharge in June 1946.

Ed taught accounting and, after retiring, he volunteered at a hospital and played music for nursing home residents. He truly is a serviceman for life.

ETHEL BURKE LATROBE, PA

TOGETHER AT LUZON

DURING WORLD WAR II, I served my first two years in the ground service of the Army Air Force and then was transferred to the infantry as part of the large number of replacements needed after the Battle of the Bulge.

After that, I went to the Philippines, where a great concentration of troops was gathering for the anticipated invasion of Japan. My camp was just outside Manila. One Saturday night, I got a letter.

It was from my brother Lester, whom I'd not seen in two years and who was stationed with a medical unit in New Guinea (his commanding officer was Dr. Charles W. Mayo of the famous Mayo Clinic).

At that stage of the war, the Allies were doing so well that censorship of military mail had eased. So Lester's news—that his unit was moving to Batangas on the Philippine island of Luzon—hadn't been blacked out. Batangas was only about 70 miles from Manila.

Having no assignment for the next day, Sunday, I grabbed a buddy and we set out for Batangas. We thumbed rides on 13 military vehicles and got there in six hours. After some searching, I found my brother's tent and slipped in as he was playing cards. I tapped him on the shoulder, and when he turned around and saw me, the last person he ever expected to see, the cards went flying and the table flipped over as he jumped up to welcome me. It was a great reunion.

MARVIN GERSHENFELD SHORELINE, WA

Marvin served in Europe and the Pacific in WWII. ★

FOXHOLE FIGHT

MARINE DIGS IN ON LETHAL TERRAIN.

At the time of the attack on Pearl Harbor, I was a junior at Appalachian State Teachers College (now University) in Boone, North Carolina, and on the varsity wrestling team. I joined the Marine Corps and was allowed to complete my junior year. In summer 1942, I did my basic training in South Carolina and special training in Pennsylvania. Marine Corps training was very physical, but I coped well since I was a P.E. major in college.

Soon I was called up to the 4th Marine Division at Camp Pendleton in California, steppingstone to the Pacific. I was made a corporal before we shipped out.

We landed on Iwo Jima on Feb. 19, 1945. On the night of the 22nd, I was wounded during an attack on the northern part of the island. Three of us were in the foxhole—two at the machine guns—and we'd used all of our ammunition. I took a group of about six men back to the depot, where we loaded boxes of ammo and hand grenades and then returned to our position. We had to step around the dead. That was the worst part.

> THREE OF US WERE IN THE FOXHOLE— TWO AT THE MACHINE GUNS—AND WE'D USED ALL OF OUR AMMUNITION.
>
> ★

I threw grenades all night. All three of us were wounded, but I considered myself lucky to be alive and taken off the island.

Wonderful medics came to help us. One gave me a disarmed Japanese grenade he'd retrieved from our foxhole. They took us to the battleship. From my bed I could see the U.S. flag after it was raised on Mount Suribachi.

I received a Bronze Star. As soon as I healed, I was sent back for the invasion of Japan, but luckily, the war ended before that happened. My last duty was guarding Japanese POWs on Guam.

I went back on the USS *Bon Homme Richard*. We were aboard on Nov. 10, 1945, the 170th anniversary of the Marine Corps, so we received a special dinner.

After I was discharged in 1946, I worked in Washington, D.C., for a few months before returning to school and my wrestling career. In four years of competing, I won two AAU championships and was defeated only once.

In 2000, I was inducted into the Appalachian State Athletics Hall of Fame.

WARREN AUSTIN SANFORD, NC

A VERY LONG DAY

NIGHT BRINGS RELIEF AFTER TENSE HOURS IN THE FIELD.

As a military policeman in a traffic squad of the 89th Infantry Division, I was often the only MP assigned to an intersection or area. Traffic section MPs usually work alone or in pairs, so it can take time to get to know your fellow soldiers. And I was assigned to the 89th only the day before it was committed to combat.

Shortly after we crossed the Rhine in March 1945, we had the Germans on the run. We were moving fast, covering as many as 40 miles a day. We often passed pockets of the enemy, making the "front" a loosely defined area instead of a line. At this time, many German troops realized the war was lost. Their morale was low, so most of the isolated units gave up without too much fight. A few, especially if embedded with SS men, didn't surrender.

Early one afternoon Cpl. Millard dropped me off at an intersection to give directions for some expected troop traffic. He left me with just my rifle, several clips of ammo and my canteen, saying he'd pick me up in a couple of hours. Surrounded by open fields, I could hear small-arms fire nearby.

I waited for hours. The expected traffic never appeared and neither did Cpl. Millard. Without rations, I was hungry. Worse, I was by myself in an exposed position in enemy territory. At the Rhine crossing, under enemy fire, my adrenaline was pumping and I was too busy to think about anything but the task at hand. Here I had nothing to do but think about my situation.

I was about to seek shelter for the night when Cpl. Millard showed up. He offered no explanation, but I'm sure he'd forgotten about me. When we reached the billet area, he said I should go to the mess tent. It was a mile up the road, and I was tired. I said I'd rather just get some sleep.

"Get something to eat," he said. "That's an order."

Looking back, his behavior may sound harsh, but I think Cpl. Millard worried he'd be in trouble for picking me up late.

After serving in Europe, Clair waited to be sent to the Pacific.

He didn't want to make it worse by having it seem as if he had kept me from having a meal. It would have been nice, though, if the corporal had offered to drive me over to the mess tent. Perhaps if he knew me better, he would have.

There was one cook still on duty, and he'd just finished cleaning up. He was reluctant to give me any food until I explained my situation. So he offered me a cheese sandwich, which I ate quickly and gratefully with some coffee.

My hunger gone, I went outside again, looking forward to a good sleep. I had survived another day.

CLAIR P. LYONS ERIE, PA

DEVOTION UNDER FIRE

A CHILDHOOD ACCIDENT LEFT MY FATHER, Anthony Massa, blind in one eye. He was rejected for military service three times until he was drafted in 1943. Because of his disability, he was assigned to the 316th Medical Battalion. His unit landed in North Africa and then Italy as part of the 5th Army under Gen. Mark Clark. My father acted as an Italian interpreter for the general a few times.

But his bravest moment occurred on July 2, 1944, near the Tuscan village of Casole d'Elsa. My father's Bronze Star citation details his actions: "Private Massa volunteered to assist in the evacuation of several wounded left behind in a house when our infantry was forced to withdraw. Although under constant enemy artillery and mortar fire; and the area being lit up from time to time by aerial flares, he continued to push forward. ... The prompt evacuation undoubtedly helped in the recovery of the wounded."

My father said that at one point that night, as he and his companions ran back with a wounded soldier, an alarm clock one of the medics found in a farmhouse suddenly sounded. The medic frantically tried to silence it as dust from bullets kicked up around my father's feet.

NICK MASSA GREEN BROOK, NJ

Art Postel spent time with Marian while on leave during WWII. ★

Pfc. Massa receives the Bronze Star from Lt. Col. Paul Brecher of the 316th Medical Battalion. ★

THREE CAME HOME

They were best friends—my brother Art, Curt Wagner, Bud Braunlich and Bill Weston. All were at school together in Davenport, Iowa, but when the war came, they went in different directions. Three joined the Navy. Art was a Seabee in Guam, Curt served in the South Pacific and Bud was in the invasion of Iwo Jima. Bill joined the Army and went to France.

Art did his best to keep up with his buddies. In November 1944, he wrote to Bill: "It sure will be swell when we can get together again and talk things over. Remember how the four of us used to go to the show on Saturday night?"

My brother's letter was returned unopened. Bill was killed in action on Dec. 3, 1944. All four went to war ready to give the last full measure of devotion. One did; three survived.

MARIAN POSTEL SCOTT SAN ANTONIO, TX

HARROWING SPOT ON WARSHIP

FIRSTHAND LOOK AT YOUNG SAILOR'S LIFE BELOW DECKS.

My father, Edward Carll, served in the Navy from 1942 to 1946 and was a crew member on the USS *Massachusetts*, deployed to the Pacific. He was on the crew for a 16-inch gun, the largest weapon on the ship. Since Edward was only 17, his father, Charles, had to sign the papers that allowed him to enlist, much to the distress of his mother, Ethel.

Edward was very skinny and could easily fit through the small hatches, so he was stationed way down on the lower deck where the powder and shells were loaded and sent up to the gun on the top deck via elevators. Being on one of the lower decks meant that he had little chance of survival if the ship was hit.

Dad met my mom, Ann, at Old Orchard Beach, Maine, when he and a Navy buddy were on leave. My parents married in 1945, while Dad was still in the Navy.

When my dad returned from the service he tried his hand at a few things, and eventually learned steel rule die making. He was one of the few people still practicing the craft in the '60s and '70s. One of his last jobs was assembling CNC milling machines at a company in Hopkinton, Massachusetts. He helped me get a job there, which launched my career as an engineer.

Dad always spoke proudly of his time in the service. In 1965, our family was present when the *Massachusetts* was brought out of mothballs to be restored as a memorial and a museum—I was 9 and remember being so proud. My wife and I have taken our children and grandchildren to see the ship docked in Battleship Cove in Fall River, Massachusetts. Recently I watched a Navy training film that must have been like what Dad saw when he was trained. I imagined him as a teenager, sitting with other recruits, learning about his assigned role on the ship.

Throughout his life, my dad kept in touch with a former crewmate, Jack Becker. They got together every year or so until my dad died in 1996.

STEVE CARLL RAYMOND, ME

Edward served on a battleship that was later preserved as a memorial. He met future wife, Ann, while on leave. ★

ONE MAN PLAYS MANY PARTS

SOLO PERFORMANCE IN HOME THEATER ENTERTAINED THE ENTIRE FAMILY.

During the Depression, ours was one of the many poor families living in Chicago, Illinois. There wasn't enough money for everyone to go to a movie, so my clever brothers and sisters saved their pennies to send the oldest, Jack, to the theater. He'd watch the movie, sometimes more than once, memorizing the storyline and as much of the dialogue as he could. When he came home, my eight siblings sat as if they were in a movie theater, and Jack would begin movie night.

Jim might act a part, or—if Jack needed a stunt person—Terry; my sisters Vernone and Rose sometimes played female roles. Most of the time, Jack acted out everything by himself, so that the family could sit back and enjoy the show. He ran, climbed and fell, and had sword fights, fistfights and arguments.

His villains brought to mind the biggest, meanest guys. His heroes and heroines were the handsomest and most beautiful Jack's audience could imagine. The show was funnier, scarier and more exciting for taking place in the minds of my brothers and sisters.

When the "movie" ended, his audience wanted more: "Play the movie again, Jack." And Jack, being the trouper that he was, would start over with a second showing.

Back then, movies opened with a newsreel, and then a cartoon. Jack skipped those parts. Only Mel Blanc could do a cartoon properly, and the news of the day wasn't very good.

I know about this family entertainment from the stories my siblings told me. I wasn't born until 1942, and Jack went off to fight in World War II, where he died in combat when I was only 2. I'm sure Jack's movies were much better than the ones shown in the theater, and I'd give anything to have been in attendance, even as an usher.

I'd love to be able to tell a story the way Jack did, although I'm not sure my children or grandchildren would be all that thrilled to hear my movie renditions.

Sometimes when I'm watching a movie that isn't very good, I think of Jack, and wonder how he'd have acted it out.

PATRICK D. HARTIGAN TORRANCE, CA

An assembler works on a B-25 bomber in the engine department of
North American Aviation in Inglewood, CA, in 1942. ★

PLAN FOR VICTORY: MAKE MORE, FASTER

FDR'S "ARSENAL OF DEMOCRACY" WAS AN UNPRECEDENTED RESHAPING OF THE AMERICAN ECONOMY TO FIGHT WWII.

A dietary condition prevented my father, Stanley, from serving in the military. Instead, he spent World War II working at the Badger Army Ammunition Plant in Sauk County, Wisconsin, making powders for hand grenades and bullets, and propellant for rockets. The 7,400-acre facility operated around the clock and housed as many as 8,000 workers and their families.

After the war, my father's experience working with and mixing chemicals helped him land a job with a fertilizer manufacturer, where he worked until he retired in 1984.

It was not until his retirement party that I thought to ask him about his wartime duties. I was at the midpoint of my own career as a supply chain manager for the refrigerator maker Greenville Products and wanted to know how inventory was managed and production was scheduled before computers.

Dad chuckled at my question. "We never paid attention to anything like that," he told me. "We had just one instruction: Make as much as you can as fast as you can."

That made a grim kind of sense. As President Franklin D. Roosevelt said, "Powerful enemies must be outfought and outproduced." We had to do everything faster than the enemy.

The most dangerous part of the job, Dad said, was loading powder into transport vehicles. The loading equipment was steel, as were the transport vehicles. The smallest spark could cause an explosion that would destroy a huge area. For safety, powder was stored in bunkers spaced over a quarter-mile apart.

War rationing affected Dad's farm family less than others because they raised their own food. But rubber was rationed. So when his old tires gave out, Dad had to take tires off one of his family's older cars.

Somehow, people got through the war on bald tires. It was as if the tires knew they had to last for the duration, Dad said.

My company had a few old-timers who had worked there during the war. Their stories were similar to my father's. They recalled how the factory had transitioned from making refrigerators to gliders in a matter of days.

The government bought all they could produce and paid on time. The men objected when the factory had to hire women, but quickly changed their minds when they saw the women work.

At the end of the war, America had mountains of war surplus. Most towns had a surplus store that sold the excess material from all branches of the military.

I was in elementary school in the early 1950s and the Army surplus store in Whitewater, Wisconsin, was a favorite place for me and my friends to hang out and shop.

Of course, none of us realized then that all the neat stuff selling so cheaply in that shop was deadly serious business to our parents' generation.

RANDALL SCHAEFER HASTINGS, MI

> THE MEN OBJECTED WHEN THE FACTORY HAD TO HIRE WOMEN, BUT QUICKLY CHANGED THEIR MINDS WHEN THEY SAW THE WOMEN WORK.

Best friends Dottie (A for Army) and Kathleen (F) thanked the Army Air Force. ★

BOND GIRLS

FOR SOME, THE BEST WAY TO HELP BRING AN END TO THE WAR WAS WITH A FRIENDLY SMILE AND A WAVE.

A s young girls, my two sisters, Dianne and Joanne, and I enjoyed going through Mom's old photo albums. There were lots of photos of our mom at events in Washington, D.C., during World War II, as well as newspaper clippings about her. We learned that our mother, Kathleen Broderick Panzone, was a "sweater girl" for the rallies that advertised war bonds. It was very exciting—our mother was a celebrity!

She began working at the Treasury Department when she was 19. In her D.C. office, beautiful and engaging women were chosen to attend the publicity rallies advertising war bond campaigns and participate in the photo shoots.

As staff members in the War Finance Program, the women had the title of War Finance Committee workers. My mom's best friend, Dorothy Heiss Artley, was in the campaigns, too. (Dottie became my godmother.)

The women were spotlighted riding in military vehicles and posing with prominent members of the military and the War Finance Committee. Sometimes they advertised the war bonds by wearing sweaters with individual letters on them spelling out a word.

Before my parents married, my dad, Domenick Panzone Jr., often attended the events, too, and told my sisters and me stories of all the hoopla and excitement at the rallies.

Dad was in the Army during the war, and both he and Mom talked about their memories of rationing. We were impressed that the entire country bonded together and gave up things, like food items and clothing, that had been a normal part of life for them before the war. Mom particularly remembered the scarcity of nylon and silk stockings. We loved to hear their stories of the sacrifices back home, and how they were vital in keeping our military supplied with everything they needed to fight and win.

After the war, Mom received an award from the Treasury Department citing her distinguished service on behalf of the War Finance Program.

When I look at these photos, I can only imagine the excitement my mom must have felt being chosen to represent the Treasury Department at such a time. The women look so eager and so full of smiles; it's difficult to comprehend that they were so very young.

I am very proud that my loving, caring and beautiful mom was instrumental in aiding the war effort.

LINDA A. PANZONE WESTMINSTER, MD

THE DAY SHE WAS WAITING FOR

HER PHOTOS REMINDED MARINE OF HOME.

Maxine Chamberlin, my mother-in-law, married her husband, Wayne, in Washington, Iowa, when they were both 19. A little more than a year after their marriage, Japan attacked Pearl Harbor on Dec. 7, 1941.

In the months that followed, millions volunteered or were drafted into the military. Wayne enlisted in the Marines and, after special training, his unit was sent to the South Pacific for the invasion of the Japanese-occupied Marshall Islands.

After Wayne shipped out, Maxine got a job at a factory in San Diego, California, manufacturing parts for the war effort. Like nearly all of the employees who were taking over the men's jobs while they were gone, she became a regular Rosie the Riveter.

Maxine didn't see Wayne for the next four years. But while he was overseas, he wrote to her often, setting up his desk with her pictures in a small folding leather frame. The couple developed a secret code to keep their letters from being censored.

After the war ended, the day finally came when Wayne was scheduled to come home. On Christmas Eve 1945, Maxine and Wayne's brother, Dallas, waited at the Washington depot for hours. Maxine had heard that by putting an ear to the rails, a listener could detect vibrations of a train from 5 miles away. She and Dallas checked again and again, and at last, after midnight, they heard the train. Maxine never forgot the joy of seeing Wayne after waiting four long years.

As soon as Wayne came back, the couple started a family. Wayne never talked much about the war with his three sons, but Maxine saved all of his letters in a cedar chest.

BECKY CHAMBERLIN LINCOLN, NE

Wayne wrote Maxine frequently. Days would pass without any mail from him, and then she'd get several letters in a pack.

FOUR WHIRLWIND DATES

THEN ROMANCE SLOWS TO THE MAIL'S PACE.

As World War II started, my mom, Henrietta Ratay, and her sister and brothers headed from Omaha, Nebraska, to California, looking for work in the war industries. Mom was hired by the telephone company and transferred to Santa Catalina Island, several miles off the Southern California coast.

Catalina became a top-secret outpost for training and early warning of attack: The U.S. Maritime Service, the Coast Guard, the Army Signal Corps and others had units on the island. The island was closed to tourists, and travel back and forth was by the SS *Catalina*—known as the Great White Steamer—so it was vital for the people on Catalina to find recreational activities on the island.

My dad, Gerald Page, lived in Santa Ana and worked for the State of California. When he received a poor draft rating due to a childhood illness, he joined the American Red Cross, and was stationed on Catalina Island.

My parents met when they were both horseback riding in the backcountry of the island. But without much warning, Dad was transferred to Adak, Alaska. From there, he wrote love letters and sent cards to my mom.

Mom moved back to Omaha, where she worked for the war department. The war was winding down and Dad wrote that he was coming to Omaha. After meeting Mom's parents, Dad returned to California and mailed an engagement ring to her.

When I was grown, Mom admitted that almost all of their dating was by mail. She thought it would set a bad example for us kids if we knew she and Dad only had four dates before he was sent to Alaska. They were married 54 years.

MARI PAGE FOUNTAIN VALLEY, CA

Newlyweds Dick and Doris, two weeks after he returned from serving in Europe, but before he got her letter.

ONE FOR THE DEAD LETTER OFFICE

SOLDIER GETS HOME AHEAD OF HIS MAIL.

My parents, the Walthers, lived across the street from Roy and Pat Hoffman in the mid-1940s. Roy's brother, William Richard—called Dick by everyone—was in the Army, and home on furlough.

One day, Dick's niece crossed the street to tell me that her uncle wanted to meet me. I told her that he should come over himself if he wanted to meet me. The girl came back a few more times, and the last time, she grabbed my shoe and took it with her. Soon Dick and Pat, his sister-in-law, brought my shoe back—and that's how I met him.

He invited me for ice cream— I said "No, thank you"—but while I was sitting on the porch later, he came back again. He had only three days left on leave, and we began dating.

Dick was in paratrooper training, and he came home once more before he was sent overseas to Germany. We got engaged while he was home, and then he was gone for a year.

> WE GOT ENGAGED WHILE HE WAS HOME, AND THEN HE WAS GONE FOR A YEAR.
>
> ★

During that time, I stopped writing him, and eventually I sent him a Dear John letter to end the relationship.

In 1946, on the day he was coming home, I was waiting tables at a local cafe. I was worried about the letter I'd sent, but when he came into the restaurant and I saw his boots, I fell in love all over again. We were married two weeks later, on March 3, 1946.

A couple of weeks after our wedding, the Dear-John letter arrived. Dick told me that if he'd known about the letter, he would have gone to Tijuana instead of coming home.

Dick and I were married for 72 years. We adopted a boy, Larry, and I now have grandchildren and a great-granddaughter. Dick died in 2018, and I miss him—he was a great husband, father, grandfather and friend. And it all started with a shoe.

DORIS F. HOFFMAN WHEATLAND, WY

PATRIOTIC PRODUCTS

Advertisers quickly capitalized on wartime changes in the 1940s, using likenesses of service personnel to sell everything from beverages to cigarettes.

Never far from Home

Coca-Cola assured soldiers they'd see the company's familiar logo in their travels and would feel like they'd run into an old friend.

Share a Sip with a Serviceman

Celebrities encouraged those on the home front to buy war bonds. Betty Grable made her pitch while promoting Royal Crown Cola and her new film *Pin-Up Girl*.

New Yorkers whoop it up on Victory over Japan Day, Aug. 14, 1945, which marked the end of the Pacific campaign in World War II. The woman held aloft has V-J Day written on her forehead. The official war's end was on Sept. 2, when Japan signed the unconditional surrender aboard the USS *Missouri*. ★

FROM OVER THERE TO RIGHT HERE

YOUNG TELEPHONE OPERATOR CONNECTS WITH RETURNING SOLDIERS.

I n June 1946, I turned 17, just in time to qualify for a summer job as a long-distance telephone operator with Pacific Bell Telephone in Oakland, California. The company recruited workers at my high school in Oakland, and the hourly wage was terrific—much better than what I was paid at the naval supply base where I'd worked the previous summer.

With but a week's training, I had to figure out call routes, take collect calls, distinguish sounds of different deposited coins and reach long-distance operators all over the United States.

Often calls went to rural areas with party lines that required sequences of different rings.

Every workday was exciting and sometimes emotionally charged. One particular day I'll never forget: I handled calls from a phone booth at a naval base where a large troop ship carrying returning servicemen docked. A long line of troops gathered at the booth, waiting to call home—some for the first time in years.

Calls were heart-wrenching. For collect calls, I needed to stay on the line to verify that I had reached the right party, which meant I heard the reactions of callers at either end as they connected. There was often so much drama and emotion in the bits of beginning communication that tears streamed down my cheeks and I struggled to keep my voice under control.

Many times I felt as if I was acting a role in a real-life movie.

The callers sometimes flirted with me and wanted my name, which wasn't allowed, but it helped to relieve my tension. Others asked what time I got off work. I'm sure I was the first American girl that some had talked with in a long while. It was a memorable job.

Three years later, I married a returned soldier who'd fought with the Rainbow Division at the Battle of the Bulge. Frank and I met at San Jose State College; the GI Bill helped him get a leg up on his career and made it possible for a young couple to survive on a tight budget. That bill provided our caring nation with a hundredfold payback.

Frank and I were married for 63 years at the time of his death.

JEANNE HAMM MACHADO SAN JOSE, CA

Jeanne shared in the joy of servicemen calling home after WWII.

Joe Natale was an ensign aboard the USS *Charrette* during WWII. ★

CALM AFTER THE STORM

My dad served on the USS *Charrette*, a destroyer that was involved in many Pacific battles. On Aug. 1, 1945, the *Charrette* and another destroyer captured the Japanese ship *Tachibana Maru*, which was masquerading as a hospital ship to smuggle soldiers and arms back to Japan.

After its last battle, during its voyage home, the *Charrette* suffered heavy damage from three typhoons. A tugboat towed the ship to Hawaii, then to Washington for repairs. It was sent out again to clean up after the war and finally sailed home in December.

Dad told me once how much he admired Japanese culture. I was so proud of him for saying that. He died in 2015, almost to the day of the 70th anniversary of the *Tachibana Maru* capture.

JULIE MANN CENTENNIAL, CO

AT NEW YORK'S V-J DAY TICKER TAPE PARADE IN 1945, SPECTATORS THREW AN UNPRECEDENTED 5,438 TONS OF PAPER, MORE THAN 100 TIMES THE AMOUNT THROWN FOR THE PARADE CELEBRATING THE NEW YORK GIANTS' SUPER BOWL VICTORY IN 2008.

★

JOINING THE FUN

WORLD WAR II HAD ENDED, and in 1946 we were coming home from the Pacific. We were given a 24-hour pass to go and celebrate at the United Service Organizations center in San Francisco, California.

While there, I joined this bunch of guys at a table. Some women in the next booth sat up to have their picture taken with us. We were clearly having a great time, but I am sorry to say that after all these years I have lost all their names.

I am the one at the far left side of the picture—the guy with all the hair!

RAYMOND K. DITE MORRIS, IL

Victory made fast friends of returning servicemen and the women at the next table at a USO celebration in 1946. ★

Winfred took this picture of three Czech villagers on the day the war in Europe ended.

SILENCE IS GOLDEN

A SMALL MEAL SHARED IN THE FIRST MOMENTS OF PEACE.

I was a combat soldier, a medic, in the front lines on May 8, 1945, walking with my fellow troops along a village road in Czechoslovakia. We were taking back the country from the Germans. We could see the villagers peeking out of their windows, looking us over. The Czechs, like so many in war-torn areas, were suffering from hunger and poverty. We didn't know it then, but that would prove to be the last day of the war in Europe.

We had been feeling it coming for a while. We crazy American kids had been taking bets about who would survive the war. We were just having fun with each other—because, of course, we didn't want harm to come to any of us.

We were walking along that small road when we heard voices screaming to us.

"Hold your position! Hold your position!"

We stopped and sat in the grass. It was a warm day; the sun was shining. Someone near me spoke: "The war is over."

We just sat there looking at each other, some looking through tears. We were quiet— no celebration, no noise, just silent stares.

The villagers in their homes across the road grew restless, walking from house to house and then turning to watch us again. I am not sure how long we sat there, but it was at least two hours.

Then some Czech women walked over and gave us sandwiches they'd made for us—tiny ham sandwiches. It was plain fare, just bread and meat. We realized they were feeding us from their meager food supplies.

Behind us was the rest of the 90th Infantry Division. These boys had landed on the beaches at Normandy and had been fighting for 11 months. The little sandwiches wouldn't have stretched to feed all of them, but no matter.

We heard voices calling to us again, softer this time, telling us to return to the last town.

The authorities put us up in local houses with civilians. We slept on the floor, wherever we could find room, grateful that it wasn't a foxhole—not that night, and not ever again.

For us, May 8, 1945, came to a quiet and peaceful close.

WINFRED HARTMAN MESA, AZ

DANCING IN THE PARK

WHEN YOU'RE THIS HAPPY, THE ONLY THING TO DO IS FORM A CONGA LINE.

Sometime between lunch and dinner, our pickup baseball game was interrupted by a blowing car horn and someone yelling down the street. It was mid-August 1945, and I was 11 years old.

Coming down the street toward us was a soldier sitting on a car's roof, his feet planted on the hood. He was waving an arm and shouting at the top of his voice. We had just been able to make out the words "war" and "over" when the air raid siren blared. That was unusual. It was only 3 p.m.—we were used to hearing that sound only at night when blackouts were in effect. To top it off, all the church bells began to peal. There were at least nine churches in Cambria City, which was our small section of Johnstown, Pennsylvania.

Putting all of these oddities together, we realized that World War II was over! To our young minds, Pope Pius XII was always the pope, Franklin Delano Roosevelt was always president (until recently, anyway) and WWII was always a daily worry.

All of us, without a word, ran—no, sprinted—home to tell our mothers and fathers the news. Getting up the block became cumbersome as folks ran out of their front doors and filled the sidewalks and streets, their mouths open in screams of jubilation. This was chaos—a very happy chaos.

When I finally did get back home, my parents were locking up our store and heading to the house. Mom shouted to me as I came in earshot.

"We heard it on the radio!"

Soon we were all heading uptown to Johnstown's Central Park, where people hugged each other and sang songs. Some of them danced in conga lines that snaked around trees, benches and water fountains.

The next day was V-J Day, and it was a total amazement. Mom opened the store at 6 a.m., and by 7:30 she was sold out of crepe paper and toilet paper. Outside people were stringing the paper everywhere—over telephone lines, up light poles, across porches and through alleyways.

Looking back, I know I was fortunate to have lived through those momentous days. Only a few months before we were in despair after President Roosevelt's death. Our community lived in constant fear that local steel mills would be bombed.

Suddenly, we were ecstatic. The relief was overpowering.

TONY PEJACK YUCAIPA, CA

> ALL OF US, WITHOUT A WORD, RAN—NO, SPRINTED—HOME TO TELL OUR MOTHERS AND FATHERS THE NEWS.

Residents of Oak Ridge, Tennessee, hold up "extra" editions of *The Knoxville Journal* on Victory over Japan Day. Oak Ridge was built in 1942 as part of the Manhattan Project, which developed atomic bombs dropped on Japan in August 1945. ★

'ONE MORE TOUR, WITH HONOR'

HONOR FLIGHTS BEGAN AS A WAY to give veterans of WWII free flights to Washington, D.C., to visit the national war memorial.

★ In 2005, Earl Morse in Ohio and Jeff Miller in North Carolina each formed organizations to fly WWII vets to the capital.

★ In 2007, Morse and Miller joined forces to form the Honor Flight Network, now with 130 hubs in 45 states, and serving veterans of WWII, Korea and Vietnam. Its motto: "One more tour, with honor." By the end of 2019, more than 245,000 veterans had gone on Honor Flights.

★ In 2008, Morse and Miller were awarded the Presidential Citizens Medal for their service to so many American veterans.

FULL DRESS

During WWII, I served in antiaircraft with Gen. George Patton's 3rd Army in Europe. When I got home in 1945, I was encouraged to keep my officer's uniform, so we carefully stored it through the years. On my Honor Flight out of Louisville in 2015, I was embarrassed at first because I was the only one in complete uniform. However, it worked out fine. In Washington, we received a special book about each memorial; I treasure it. I can't say enough of what I felt seeing the memorials. I was a platoon commander in the war, and I recalled the young men who served with me and ones left behind. In this picture, I'm at the Korean War memorial wall.

JOHN B. STONE BOWLING GREEN, KY

STANDING FOR ANOTHER

Al Taylor, my father-in-law, served in WWII, but he resisted taking an Honor Flight until 2014, when he agreed to go bearing a picture of my friend's father, Calvin Hake, a Marine veteran who had recently died. Dad chuckled at an Army man representing a Marine, but the trip meant a lot to him. He appreciated the sailor thanking him for his service and the more than 300 letters he received during the flight's mail call.

ROSANNE TAYLOR WEST CHESTER, PA

STATESIDE SERVICE ⌃

My granddaughter Sarah Prohuska was my guardian on my Honor Flight in September 2019. During WWII, I was a secretary at the Naval Annex, part of the Congressional liaison serving the Navy and Marines. I handled letters from parents writing to officials on behalf of their children on active duty, which meant I was at the West Wing of the White House almost every day. I still have my security badge from that time.

EVELYN McNEILL SCOTT GRAFTON, WI

PROUD TO BE COUNTED ⌄

From the moment I got to Midway Airport in Chicago, I was treated like a king. There were about 100 other veterans on the flight to D.C. At the capital, we were welcomed by firefighters giving us a water-cannon salute, and at each memorial there were servicemen and servicewomen and musicians to greet us. On the flight home, we had a mail call with letters from family, friends and schoolchildren, all thanking us for our service. For me, this part of the trip really put the "honor" in Honor Flight. It was without doubt one of my proudest days.

I served with the 101st Airborne in the Korean War.

I'm second from left in this picture. With me are Bob Sousa (left), Al Filafusi and Don Miller.

JAMES C. TERPSTRA ROSELLE, IL

VETERAN HELPING VETERAN «

On an Honor Flight in 2017, I escorted John McAlpine, a WWII veteran who served in the Navy, on our trip to Washington, D.C. I am also a veteran, having served in Vietnam.

John and I visited many sites, but we spent considerable time at the World War II memorial and the Vietnam Veterans Memorial wall.

John is now an active member of the New York State American Legion, McKeever Post 64.

ROBERT J. KENEFIC HAMBURG, NY

NEWS FROM THE FRONT

REPORTERS DIVE INTO HARM'S WAY WITH ONLY A PEN, A CAMERA AND A PASSION FOR TRUTH.

BY **MARY-LIZ SHAW**

EDWARD R. MURROW
1908-1965

BORN IN RURAL NORTH CAROLINA and raised in Washington state, Edward R. Murrow had a talent for organization and managing people—he should have had a respectable career as a media administrator. Instead, he became one of the most trusted voices of early broadcast journalism.

His foray into reporting occurred in 1937, while he was head of CBS' European operations. Germany invaded Austria, and Murrow rushed to cover it. From then on, aided by a cadre of talented reporters known as the Murrow Boys—among them Eric Sevareid, Howard K. Smith, William L. Shirer and one woman, Mary Marvin Breckinridge—he detailed in cogent dispatches the brunt of the European conflict for American listeners.

During the 1940 London Blitz, when Germany bombed the English capital for 57 straight nights, Murrow spoke from the teetering rooftops and blasted avenues of a great city that was down but not out. In one, he told of piercing sirens and smoke billowing over the streets; in another, of "the red, angry snap of antiaircraft guns."

Murrow was credited with helping to turn American opinion away from isolationism to joining the fight.

From London, Ed Murrow brought the reality of Hitler's onslaught in Europe into American living rooms. ★

DICKEY CHAPELLE
1919-1965

FIDEL CASTRO CALLED HER the "polite little American with all that tiger blood in her veins." Dickey Chapelle, indeed little at just 5 feet, pursued her work with a nerve as steely as the Marines she admired. In 1945, she talked her way onto Iwo Jima, where she promptly climbed a hill to snap the battle amid the annoying buzzing of wasps. She realized later those wasps were bullets.

For the next 20 years, Chapelle reported on conflicts in hot spots around the globe, including Lebanon, Algeria, Hungary and Vietnam. In fatigues, bush hat and pearl studs, she kept up with the boys no matter what, even learning to parachute in her 40s. When a young reporter named Mike Wallace asked whether she, a woman, should be out there covering all that war, Chapelle didn't hesitate.

"It is not a woman's place, there's no question about that," she told him. "There is only one other species on earth for whom a war zone is no place, and that's men."

She died of shrapnel wounds from a tripwire mine on a search-and-destroy mission with her beloved Marines in Vietnam. They dedicated a plaque in her name near the place where she fell: "She was one of us and we will miss her."

★ Chapelle's favorite picture of herself. Marine Master Sgt. Len Lowery took it during the opening of the St. Lawrence Seaway in 1959.

ERNIE PYLE
1900-1945

THE ONLY SON OF INDIANA TENANT FARMERS, Ernie Pyle was humble and soft-spoken, but his quiet manner hid a powerful longing for adventure. Early on, Pyle saw journalism as a way of satisfying his wanderlust, but it wasn't the only way: At varying points, he was an oil field worker, cabin boy and freighter hand.

In the mid-1930s, he was managing editor of the *Washington Daily News* in D.C. when he conceived his own dream job: roving the globe and writing about the people he met. He kept up a punishing pace, filing six columns a week, until by 1940, he estimated he had covered 200,000 miles and written 1.5 million words. His syndicated columns gained him millions of readers. When he reached London to cover the war in Europe, his natural, friendly way earned him the trust of troops and civilians, which gave him unique insights on the effects of the conflict on ordinary folk. In detailed, sympathetic reports, he told of the resiliency of Londoners and, later, of the bravery of American infantrymen.

Pyle covered battles in North Africa, Italy and France, winning the Pulitzer in 1944. On April 18, 1945, while with the 77th Infantry on the Okinawa campaign, he was killed by enemy fire on the island of Ie Shima.

★ Ernie Pyle shares a companionable moment with troops during the Pacific campaign in 1945.

★ This portrait of Margaret Bourke-White in full air gear became an unlikely popular pinup during WWII.

MARGARET BOURKE-WHITE
1904-1971

ONE OF THE FIRST PHOTOGRAPHERS hired for the fledgling *Life* magazine in the mid-1930s, Margaret Bourke-White had an easy grace and an artist's eye for composition. She made her name as a chronicler of the industrial age. But she found purpose and a mission traveling with writer Erskine Caldwell through the South, documenting the working poor of the Great Depression.

Covering World War II, Bourke-White displayed uncommon empathy for the human cost of conflict. In 1941, she was the first woman to fly on a B-17 bombing raid, and the only Westerner in Moscow when the Germans invaded. She crossed Germany with Gen. George S. Patton in 1945 as his army liberated concentration camps.

Bourke-White went on to photograph India's independence movement, the effects of apartheid in South Africa and the Korean War, but finally shuttered her camera in 1957 due to Parkinson's disease.

Mike Conrad in Vietnam in 1970. His wife sent the picture after Nancy shared a copy of Mike's letter.

PEN PAL IN VIETNAM

READING OLD LETTER OPENS NEW DOORS.

A s elementary students in 1970, we didn't know what it meant that there was a war in Vietnam. There were protests and demonstrations on college campuses opposing the war, but our class of third graders in Racine, Wisconsin, wrote letters to the brave, unknown soldiers fighting across the globe.

My letter went to Mike Conrad, who was serving in the 101st Airborne. I was so excited when I got a response from Mike. It came in an airmail envelope personally addressed to me.

Recently, I found the letter, dated Jan. 26, 1970. He thanked me for writing: "It really means a lot to all of us when we get a letter." Mike told me that he was 23 and from North Carolina; he was married but didn't have kids. He explained that, in Vietnam, it was monsoon season, and told me what that meant. He also offered me some useful advice:

"I'm glad to hear that you like school. This will help you a lot in life. Because a good education is very important. Always be sure that you do your best in everything you do."

After finding the letter, I couldn't get his name out of my head. Through an online search, I found that Mike died in January 2019, but I was able to locate his wife, Becky. I wrote her and enclosed a copy of Mike's letter.

"Such a touching surprise," were Becky's words in an email back to me, "joyful and bittersweet at the same time." She sent me a photo of Mike during his service in Vietnam, a photo of their family, and a copy of my letter I had written back to Mike, dated Feb. 3, 1970. Mike obviously treasured my letter just as much as I treasured his.

> MIKE OBVIOUSLY TREASURED MY LETTER JUST AS MUCH AS I TREASURED HIS.
> ★

The letter that my third grade self composed was not too bad! I told Mike that I'd had a tooth pulled, that I was an aunt, and that I was learning to ice skate, though I was a chicken. "My mother and father send their best wishes and say they hope you will be able to come home soon," I wrote.

Becky told me that Mike died from cancer he contracted from exposure to Agent Orange. Through the stories she shared, I learned that the young man I never got to meet was an avid traveler and volunteer, and a wonderful husband, father and grandfather.

Decades after Mike and I wrote to one another, the kind letters we exchanged are still bringing people together.

NANCY MADEY HUNTINGTON BEACH, CA

★ ★ ★ LITTLE GI ★ ★ ★

My future husband, Larry, was 2 in 1942 when he posed in
his Army Air Corps uniform with his 5-year-old sister, Arline.
He grew up to join the Air Force for real.

YVONNE JANOFF BIGFORK, MT

ONE NATION

Read about early immigrants coming to find the
American dream, the struggle for civil rights and the
determination that makes up our strong character.

At far left, a girl curls up for a nap after arriving at Ellis Island on the USS *General R.M. Blatchford* with other displaced persons from Europe in 1950; eateries for just about any craveable cuisine thrive side by side on a street in Brooklyn, NY; below, Americans of different racial and ethnic backgrounds vote for president. Signing the register is Irene Louie, originally from China.

In a refugee camp in the 1940s, Zocia and her family were cared for by a troop member whose name they never knew. ★

A GUIDING HAND

YEARSLONG SEARCH FOR THE STRANGER WHO REACHED OUT TO HER.

T he autumn of 1951 found our family of five disembarking the USS *General Leroy Eltinge*, a World War II troop transport ship repurposed to bring refugees to America. We had been living in various displaced persons camps in Europe for six years.

I will never forget setting foot on land with Lady Liberty in the background, nor the sights and sounds of thousands of people shouting in different languages as we all jockeyed for position in line for immigration processing.

After the war, my mother was very ill and my father was severely traumatized. They had been captured by the Nazis, selected for hard labor and barely survived. I was born into these circumstances.

Later, both of my brothers were born in displaced persons camps. It was rare to see or hear children in those camps, especially soon after the war; many had not survived the conflict, and life in the camps could be very hard.

My brothers and I were sought after by people whose own children hadn't made it; we were played with, cooed over, cuddled, kissed and sometimes cried over before being sent back to our parents at the end of the day.

My parents spoke rarely of their experiences— which were too painful to think about. But many years later, Mother talked of the soldier in a picture she'd saved. It shows me holding his hand, both of us squinting into the sun, at the resettlement camp in Coburg, Germany. It was taken in 1946 or 1947.

This soldier, Mother told me, took us under his wing and helped our family to navigate the complicated and confusing resettlement process. At the same time, he gave us emotional and material support, offering certain little comforts as best he could until we left for our voyage to our adoptive country.

I have long wished to find out the identity of this wonderful man who—like so many men and women in the military, some of whom sacrificed their lives—gave us another chance at life. He was an important part of our journey as we sought sanctuary and a new home in the United States.

Perhaps the soldier retained a copy of the picture, and there is someone somewhere wondering about the little girl with him.

I would love for him to know that I have been searching for him these many years to thank him. At the very least, I want his family to know of his kindness to us and what a comfort he was at a time when we needed it.

This soldier and I have a special bond, and much to catch up on.

ZOCIA PAWLOWSKI BARR WILMINGTON, NC

> AT THE VERY LEAST, I WANT HIS FAMILY TO KNOW OF HIS KINDNESS TO US AND WHAT A COMFORT HE WAS AT A TIME WHEN WE NEEDED IT.

LEARNING THE ROPES, OKLAHOMA STYLE

KIND NEIGHBORS—AND ICE CREAM—EASE CULTURE SHOCK.

Klausdorf, Germany, was a relatively safe village, and my family was lucky to be able to spend the majority of World War II there. When the war ended we returned to Berlin and found our apartment house was still standing. It was located in West Berlin in the American sector.

My father died in Russia during the war and my mother, Ursula Margarete, married an American soldier, Master Sgt. S.K. Oleson. They were reassigned to Fort Sill, Oklahoma, in 1949.

My little brother, Dieter, and I arrived in Lawton, Oklahoma, two years later with my grandma, whom we called Oma. We didn't speak a word of English. In Berlin, it felt like fall, but it was hotter than blue blazes in Lawton. We hated it.

We decided to give America a chance when we met the people who lived next door. As soon as we knew Doris and Landrum Neeley, we began to call them Tante (Aunt) Doris and Onkle Skinny.

Doris and Skinny, and their friends Slick and Marguerite, became wonderful friends to my parents, and were like family to us. They taught us how to barbecue, eat corn on the cob, hand-crank ice cream and spit watermelon seeds. Dieter and I went to their house after school. Doris always had treats, hugs and kindness. When kids made fun of us, Doris went to school and put an end to it.

We remained friends with the Neeleys until Tante Doris died at 96. Their warm welcome to America made all the difference to us.

PETRA GILBERT MARQUIS ORANGE, CA

Petra's family, reunited in 1952. From left, Oma Margrete; Dieter, 8; mom Ursula Margarete; Petra, 10; and stepdad S.K. ★

ESCAPE FROM PRUSSIA

UPHEAVAL SENDS FAMILY FLEEING FOR SAFETY.

Hanna Quapp, my mother, was born in Prussia (now part of Poland) in 1933. She was raised with her brother and four sisters on a farm.

In January 1945, Russians invaded from the east. The Quapp family fled, leaving behind the farm that had been in the family for 200 years. When they reached the Baltic Sea with hundreds of other refugees, they escaped onto a German warship headed for the unknown. The ship moved out to sea surrounded by artificial fog to avoid detection from Russian torpedo boats.

The family arrived in Denmark and was assigned to a refugee camp. They survived the next two years with only basic necessities. During the harsh winters, they had little to eat.

In June 1947 they were allowed to relocate to West Germany, where the government provided them a plot of land with an abandoned army barracks for their new home.

Now a young adult, Hanna worked at the American Express office in Stuttgart, where she met and got engaged to Karl Herrmann, my father.

> MY PARENTS WERE MARRIED IN WASHINGTON, D.C., BY A PASTOR WHO SPOKE GERMAN AND ENGLISH.
>
> ★

Karl had a dream to emigrate to America. He made the long boat trip first, and settled in Arlington, Virginia. Then he saved money for Hanna's ticket, and she joined him in May 1955.

My parents were married in Washington, D.C., by a pastor who spoke German and English. Mom wore the wedding dress her sister Marianne made before she left Germany. The church provided cake and flowers, and my parents ate their wedding supper at the corner drugstore.

In time, stashing their cash in a dresser drawer, they saved enough for their first car. Dad was so proud of the black Chevy sedan that he often polished it with his handkerchief.

Dad worked for the German airline Lufthansa, and my parents raised two daughters who enjoyed the good life in America. Dad died in 1986, but Mom still travels, sews and reads with her five grandchildren, who call her Oma.

SUZY MOFFITT SOUTH BEND, IN

JOURNEY BY FAITH

THE YEAR WAS 1912, and my grandparents Karl and Anne Bredesen Westby were leaving Oslo, Norway. They wanted to join relatives in the country they'd heard called "a paradise below the western horizon."

Karl, Anne and their three children—one was my father, Irving—were scheduled to travel on a new ship called *Titanic*. However, Anne was pregnant and wasn't feeling well, so they actually traveled later than they planned.

My grandparents didn't speak English, and when they arrived in the U.S., they accidentally got on the wrong train. It took them to Montreal, Canada, where they spent a night in the railway station. Cold and hungry, they finally got to their destination in Madison, South Dakota.

Four months after their arrival, Karl died of a ruptured appendix. Anne had $22 and four children to care for. To support them, she worked for another Norwegian farmer, doing ironing and housework. They married and had three children.

My grandmother must have had a strong faith to make it through those times.

YVONNE WESTBY HILL WELLINGTON, KS

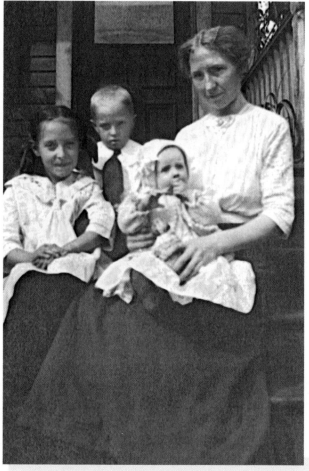

★ Anne with three of her children, Magnhild, Barney and baby Volly, a year after they reached Madison, South Dakota.

LEARNING A SECOND LANGUAGE

Erich Slotty, my father, was born in 1902 in Berlin, Germany. In 1923, accompanied by three siblings, he joined an aunt in the U.S. She paid my father's $200 fare. He reached Ellis Island after 12 days in third class on the SS *Orbita*.

His first order of business was to learn English. In the picture, he is at far left; his brother Reinhold is sitting behind him. On the chalkboard is written "English Class, Dover Street School, Milwaukee, Wisconsin, USA."

WAYNE SLOTTY UNION GROVE, WI

TEMPORARY TO PERMANENT STATUS

NOVEMBER 1956: I was a newlywed on the way to the USA onboard the beautiful RMS *Queen Mary*. I hadn't wanted to leave England or my family in Birmingham, but my husband promised we'd only stay for two years. Promises, promises.

After several job changes and living in four different states, we settled in Indiana, where we built a house, raised four children and, in 1964, became citizens. Later, we sponsored my parents and siblings to immigrate to the U.S.

While working in our local library system in Indiana, I met Sheila, a fellow Brit from Liverpool, who also came over on the *Queen Mary*, although at a different time. (See story at right.) We became fast friends and now live right next door to each other. We share memories, movies, books and magazines.

Whatever happened to those two years I was promised in '56? I'm still here, with my wonderful family, including great-grandchildren.

BERYL CHATTERTON NOBLESVILLE, IN

Sheila met Homer following his return to the U.S. after serving in the Army. ★

RMS *Queen Mary* brought Beryl, left, and Sheila to America at different times. They ended up next-door neighbors. ★

BRITISH TRANSPLANT BECOMES A REAL YANK

UNCLE BILL AND AUNT NELL sponsored me to come to the states from Liverpool, England, in 1961. I came over on the magnificent RMS *Queen Mary*. My aunt and uncle picked me up in New York at the docks and we drove to Cleveland, Ohio.

To pay my way, I worked at Kresge's dime store on the candy counter. I had to announce over the loudspeaker, "Come and get your fresh candy and nuts." They liked my British accent.

I met my husband, Homer, just after he returned from serving two years in Germany with the Army. We had three children, and I was so proud when I became a citizen in 1968. I was a real Yankee Doodle!

While working as a volunteer in the bookshop of the Noblesville Library, I met a fellow Brit who came into the shop to donate some British magazines. (See story at left.) Beryl and I started talking, and we had so much in common that we became great friends—in fact, she moved in next door to me.

SHEILA McCORMICK NOBLESVILLE, IN

READY TO ENLIST

SOLDIER SEIZES OPPORTUNITY TO SIGN UP FOR THE CITIZEN RANKS.

My brother and I were born in Italy when the country was ruled by fascist dictator Benito Mussolini. My father feared that war was coming, and so in 1936 we came to the U.S., landing in New York. Later, when I was drafted into the Army, the question of my citizenship never came up. I thought no one cared.

I was in the 45th Infantry Division in Korea in 1953. A cease-fire was holding and we all anxiously awaited orders that we'd be going home. In the meantime, passes and leaves were canceled, and routines that had gotten slack—roll call, spit-and-polish boots, calisthenics—resumed.

Then one morning I read an article in *Stars and Stripes* that said representatives from the Bureau of Immigration and Naturalization would be in Seoul accepting applications for citizenship for any service members who were not U.S. citizens.

I reported to the company commander, requesting a three-day pass to Seoul to apply for the program. His response: "If this is a scam for a pass, you'll be doing KP for a month." I waited until he calmed down before telling him I also needed three witnesses and a jeep. That didn't help his disposition.

Once in Seoul, I stated my case, and an official agreed that I qualified for citizenship.

I have fond memories of staying in Seoul for those three days—sleeping late, no roll call or inspections—but most important was receiving my certificate for citizenship to the greatest country in the world.

> I WAITED UNTIL HE CALMED DOWN BEFORE TELLING HIM I ALSO NEEDED THREE WITNESSES AND A JEEP.

FRANK NICOLAZZO ROCHESTER, NY

FASHIONABLE READY-TO-WEAR

Companies founded by immigrants set New York's garment sector booming.

Wardrobe on a Budget »

Sacony, brand name for S. Augstein & Co., was a clothier founded by Czech immigrant Siegmund Augstein in the 1890s. It specialized in women's knitted sportswear. Here, it targets students with washable wools to mix and match. "College Pointers" is a pun: Augstein was based in College Point on Long Island.

« Polyester Chic

DuPont invokes Abe Schrader, a king of New York's garment district, to sell the glories of Dacron, a textile made with its chemicals. Schrader was known for his tasteful, tony designs. He immigrated to the U.S. in 1921 after serving in the Polish army. He dashed his mother's dreams that he'd become a rabbi when he joined his uncle's clothing firm.

IRISH UNION SOLDIER

LEAVING THE FAMINE IN HIS HOMELAND, HE FOUGHT FOR THE NORTH.

T he potato crops in Ireland had several years of failures in the mid-1800s, and in 1845 the Great Famine began to ravage the country. Individuals and entire families left the country by the hundreds of thousands. Many Irish coming to the U.S. were greeted with the notice "No Irish Need Apply."

One of those immigrants was my ancestor James Deery, who landed in Brooklyn, New York. James, my great-great-great-uncle, was born in Donegal, Ireland, in 1841. He left for the U.S. via Liverpool when he was 9. Like many poor immigrants, he stayed in the place he landed.

When the Civil War broke out, James enlisted for the Union, joining the 6th Cavalry Regiment (regular army) as a private. He was at Gettysburg with his unit on July 3, 1863, the last day of the conflict. James was injured that day and received a monthly pension for the rest of his life. In 1913, he returned to Gettysburg for a reunion of the Union and Confederate soldiers.

After the war, he worked for many years for the New York City Fire Department.

Over 150 years later, I'm proud that my Irish ancestor participated in the Battle of Gettysburg, which remains one of the bloodiest and most famous battles in U.S. history.

MAUREEN KING-CASSIDY OYSTER BAY, NY

Immigrant soldiers, like those in the Irish Brigade pictured here, were well represented in the Union army. ★

Clare learned about her grandparents, Clara and Isadore Rothman, left, and Regina and Herman Rosett, through her parents' stories. ★

EMBRACE A NEW IDENTITY

GRANDPARENTS MAKE CHANGES TO HAVE A FRESH START IN AMERICA.

My grandmothers died before I was born. In the tug of war between the spirits of Regina and Clara, my parents, Leonard and Gertrude, told me many stories.

Leonard's mother, Regina, was educated in a convent in Austria-Hungary. She married her first cousin Herman Reiningstein, and they came to America in the 1890s. The first of the family to arrive, they settled in the Bronx, New York. Others followed, most of whom, like Regina and Herman, changed their name to Rosett. According to my mother, Regina always wore a baggy housedress with an apron, instead of dressing like she had a good education. Herman worked in the garment industry until he became ill. They were buried in a Brooklyn cemetery we called the Hungarian Fields.

In my mother's stories, her mother, Clara, came off the winner in comparison with Regina. Clara Velson and Isadore Ruttman were 16 when they left Odessa, Russia, in 1892. Their names were changed to Rothman at Ellis Island, and they settled in New York. Grandma Clara "dressed." She was a seamstress who loved beautiful clothes and diamonds. But she could afford only one diamond at a time. At 50, Clara proudly posed for a picture with mismatched diamonds dangling from her ears. My mother noted that Clara worked herself to death for those mismatched diamonds.

I missed meeting both my grandmothers. But it probably never entered Clara's mind that by working too hard, she would miss out on getting to dandle a granddaughter. Like Regina, life kept her too busy to think such thoughts.

CLARE GOLDFARB ATLANTA, GA

PICTURES FROM THE PAST
★ ★ ★ Land of Opportunity ★ ★ ★

COMING TO AMERICA
Displaced after the war in Europe, a boy waits with his fellow passengers on the USS *General R.M. Blatchford* at Ellis Island in New York, 1951.

JOURNEY THERE AND BACK AGAIN
My father, John J. Byrne Sr., was born in Donegal, Ireland. In the early 1900s, his parents immigrated to Butte, Montana. This photo of the family was taken there when he was 7, in 1908. His father died in a mining accident, and Dad and his mother returned to Ireland. In 1922, when Dad was 21, he came back, arriving at Ellis Island on the TSS *Columbia*. He moved to Fort Worth, where a cousin had a job waiting for him.
JOHN J. BYRNE JR. ARLINGTON, TX

WELCOME SIGHT

New citizens from Hungary turn their attention toward the Statue of Liberty in New York Harbor in 1948. Displaced by upheaval at the start of the Cold War, refugees from Eastern European countries were accepted into the U.S. as part of a relaxed immigration policy.

SEARCH FOR AFRICAN AMERICAN FAMILY HISTORY

ENSLAVED CHILD'S JOB POINTS TO LINEAGE.

As the family historian, I discovered that my great-great-grandfather, George Washington Fagan, was born in 1819 in Buckingham County, Virginia. Several facts in my sources point to George's father being the plantation owner. First, George was taught to read and write. In addition, as a youngster, his primary duty was to keep the "master's big black boots clean and shiny." Then, as a young man, he acted as a foreman for the operation of the plantation. Last, he appeared in the 1870 census under the classification "mulatto."

George's owner was in debt to a plantation owner in Albemarle County. Apparently, as part of an agreement, George and several other slaves were sent to that plantation to work off their owner's debt. Fortunately for them, the Civil War ended and the slaves were freed. Of his own free will, my great-great-grandfather stayed in Albemarle County, where the strong roots of our family tree were planted.

George's first marriage was to a woman referred to in my sources as "a Riffin girl." She died sometime after their only child, Ardelia, was born in 1847. His second marriage, to Angeline Randolph, produced 10 children—an important and dynamic branch of our family tree.

Ardelia Fagan married Harry Armstead, who during "slavery times ... was put up for sale four times." Each time, Harry's slavemaster was not satisfied with the offers he received and therefore did not sell him. The 1880 census listed Harry as a farmhand; the 1900 census showed him owning his own farm "free and clear."

Harry and Ardelia had 10 children, including my grandmother Bessie, who was born in 1890. She was able to get a third or fourth grade education and described to me how she wrote her lessons on a piece of slate. Her husband, John Washington, born in 1887, could not read or write. I remember him marking an "X" on his paychecks so that my grandmother could cash them. I discovered John in the 1900 census, where he was 13 and classified as a full-time farmhand.

Bessie and John had seven children, including my wonderful mother, Louise, born in 1923. I am the oldest of five children. Born in 1943, I am named after my great-grandfather, Harry Armstead, born 100 years earlier in 1843.

Although research indicates that some of our ancestors bore the yoke of slave experience, it also shows that they triumphed over this negative history with strength of character, religious belief and a firm commitment to self-development and survival of the family.

Our family tree has thrived because of its strong roots. Descendants of the enslaved boy who shined his master's boots have succeeded in such diverse professions as law, medicine, banking, history and research, real estate, music, the military, education and the ministry.

HARRY JAMES FORD PITTSBURGH, PA

George Washington Fagan, born on a Virginia plantation, was freed while working off the plantation owner's debt. At left, six slaves listed on the manifest from the schooner *Wild Cat* are identified by their first names only, which can make researching ancestry difficult. The ship arrived at New Orleans, LA, in 1832. ★

★ Tuskegee Airmen strategize on an aircraft wing in Tuskegee, AL, in 1943. These men, along with many others, would go on to fly 15,000 sorties from 1943 to 1945.

THE TUSKEGEE AIRMEN

IN THE DAUNTING FACE OF racial discrimination and limited opportunities for African Americans, these aviators created a record of excellence that paved the way for racial integration in the U.S. armed forces in 1948. The brave men got their name from the Tuskegee Army Air Field in Alabama, where, from 1941 to 1946, some 1,000 African American volunteers were trained as military pilots, navigators and bombardiers.

The airmen became one of the most respected and in-demand fighter groups during World War II, amassing one of the lowest loss records while escorting bombers and earning three Presidential Unit Citations.

PICTURES FROM THE PAST
★★★ Civil Rights ★★★

A TIME FOR CHANGE

Martin Luther King Jr. delivered his "I Have a Dream" speech in the nation's capital on Aug. 28, 1963—less than 10 years after the Supreme Court in 1954 ruled in *Brown v. Board of Education* that "separate but equal" laws that kept the races segregated were unconstitutional. Though Jim Crow slowly disappeared, it didn't fade fast enough. Thus was born the civil rights movement, the hallmarks of which were nonviolent civil disobedience, boycotts and voter registration drives.

The Rev. Martin Luther King Jr. (left), the Rev. Albert Brinson (center) and A.D. King received a summons for protesting at an A&P grocery store that would not hire Blacks.

STANDING UP BY SITTING DOWN

AN ACT FOR THE GREATER GOOD.

On March 15, 1960, I was a 21-year-old student at Morehouse College, an all-black school in Atlanta. On that day, I led nine students into the Union Station cafeteria and staged a sit-in. By federal law, because the train station was a public facility, anyone should have been allowed to eat there. But that was not the reality.

We arrived at 11:20 a.m., before the lunch crowd. We'd prepared ourselves to be nonviolent, should violence break out, and to carry ourselves as ladies and gentlemen.

We found an empty table and sat down. A white waitress scurried over. She snatched up the napkin holders as well as the salt and pepper shakers, leaving the table bare.

After a few minutes, the manager came over and demanded, "What do you want? You know you have no business here."

I said, "Sir, we came in to be served lunch." He stormed off, indignant and angry. I glanced toward the counter. The customers sitting there glared back. I said a silent prayer: "Dear God, work this out and keep us safe."

News must have spread quickly because outside the window, I could see the street filling with parked cars, pedestrians peering in and news photographers snapping our pictures. We sat silently amid the chaos—the humility of my younger friends is something I'll never forget.

Suddenly a police wagon pulled up outside, and an officer came in. Pointing to the manager, he said, "Mr. Teal said he told you folks that you can't eat here. So what are you going to do?"

I said, "Sir, we came here to be served, and we intend to sit here until we are served or we're told why we're not being served."

"OK, then," the officer said. "You'll have to come with me. Please stand."

We were escorted out of the restaurant, past the cameras, past the police, past the people staring and up the steps into the back of the police wagon, where we were taken to jail...all because we wanted some lunch.

REV. ALBERT BRINSON COLLEGE PARK, GA

★ ★ ★ INSPIRING A NATION ★ ★ ★

On Aug. 28, 1963, in Washington, D.C., James Atherton placed his camera on a pole and hoisted it above Abraham Lincoln's shoulder. In so doing, he captured a pivotal moment in our nation's history. At the podium below, the Rev. Martin Luther King Jr. stood before a crowd of more than 200,000 Americans who had gathered peacefully at the Lincoln Memorial. King's "I Have a Dream" speech was broadcast into millions of homes, inspiring the nation to support civil rights legislation. King's words and Atherton's photograph are as powerful today as they were decades ago.

HARD AT WORK

For first responders, farmers, volunteers in the Peace Corps and so many others, perseverance and dedication are core American values.

At far left, workers assemble control units for tanks and aircraft during World War II; welders prepare to work on the SS *George Washington Carver* in 1943; below, a flight nurse steps off a medical plane during the Korean War in 1950; and a Minnesota farmer readies a cow for milking in 1939.

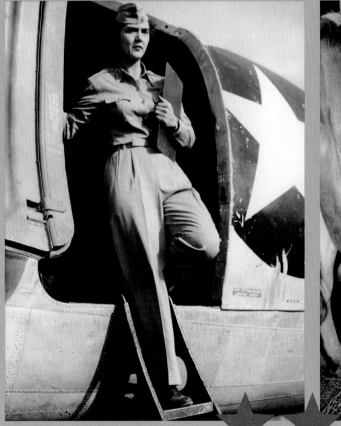

Like the author, Max Kroll served with the Peace Corps in India in the 1960s. He and his wife, Blanche, ran a clinic in this village. ★

A DIFFERENT PATH

ONCE THE IDEA TOOK HOLD, SHE SAW THE ROAD SHE WAS DESTINED TO TAKE.

When President John F. Kennedy formed the Peace Corps in 1961, I was 17. The concepts on which the Corps was based drew my attention from the beginning. In spring 1965, my graduation from Marquette University imminent, nothing drew my interest more than the Peace Corps, to my parents' dismay. That August I began training for Peace Corps groups going to Mysore state (now Karnataka) and Maharashtra state in western central India.

Our training covered public health, including nutrition, latrine building, poultry raising, kitchen gardening and many other healthy living skills. In addition, we studied the area's language and culture for several hours a day. Our teachers were from the states where we would be assigned.

My experience working on a public health project at two villages could be frustrating because of the government bureaucracy, and village problems were numerous and seemed overwhelming. But the rewards in personal relationships and insights on the world were rich and profoundly moving. As an American, a woman and a person of faith, I am who I am today in great measure because of those two years living with the villagers in India who welcomed me into their lives. Our cook, the errand-runner from the health center, the female leaders from the county level and the doctor who had a practice in the village—so many kind people had an impact on my life. And of course my fellow volunteers, who put their hearts, souls and skills into helping to change the serious health outcomes of villagers.

I look back and I wish...I wish that I had done more, that I had more knowledge, energy and time back then to effect true change. But I am grateful I chose to go on the adventure. We earned 11 cents an hour for two years, but we had an experience like no other. Without a doubt, the volunteers felt the greatest impact of the journey. India changed us more than we changed India.

MIA ADDESA KUEBLER CLARENCE, NY

Richard Monks, a 23-year-old Peace Corps volunteer, teaches math in Malaysia in 1969. ★

THERE AND BACK AGAIN

FROM THE DAKOTAS TO THE PHILIPPINES, LIFE COMES FULL CIRCLE FOR ONE FARMER.

Growing up in the Great Depression, I saw our Langdon farm forced into foreclosure. When I graduated from high school in 1943, my parents had three younger children and needed me to stay home to help buy back the farm. By 1966 my dad had passed away, and I was still here, living with my mother. Around that time, I happened to meet a Peace Corps volunteer and began to think about joining. I realized anyone could work this farm, but I wanted a chance to do something that very few ever would.

In the early 1970s, to the surprise of everyone I knew, I sold all my machinery and rented out the farm for five years. (I farmed it again after the lease ended.)

I was lucky that the Peace Corps was starting a new program that needed farmers. I left for the Philippines in 1973. I would be paid $75 a month in a pilot program that involved working with rural banks to set up loans for local farmers. There were 27 of us; I was 47, the oldest was 66 and the youngest 18.

For my first night in Naguilian, in La Union province, my assigned Filipino family cooked me a whole fish and watched me eat it. Naguilian had no electricity, limited water and no phones. It wasn't much different from how I grew up during the Depression years. I soon learned that if you went to someone's home, they would feed you even if they had very little. And they would keep feeding you until you left some food on your plate. For 75 cents, I'd take a bus 150 miles into the capital, Manila. The trip lasted all day, and the bus picked up any person who flagged it—some of them carrying chickens or pigs. We'd get into the city with people hanging off the sides. It was hot, noisy and dusty, but it never bothered me.

On one of these trips, I met Catalina (Lina) and her 2-year-old daughter, Leah. Lina and I fell in love and got married.

I had to cut my Peace Corps service short after I developed an allergy. Lina and I came home in 1974. I adopted Leah, and Lina and I had a son in 1976.

A neighbor once remarked that I must regret joining the Peace Corps. "Think of the money you could've made," he said. I have never regretted it. My wife, daughter and son are priceless. In my nineties, I am lucky to have my younger Peace Corps friends, as all my other friends have passed away.

Peace Corps volunteers join with high expectations of helping others—that's the main reason I joined—but after it's over, we find that we got as many, if not more, benefits from the experience.

DICK HAMANN LANGDON, ND

PASTRY CHEF IN THE MAKING

HIGH SCHOOL STUDENT FINDS HERSELF ON THE BUSINESS END OF A CREAM PUFF.

The minute my sisters and I got our allowances, we headed to the town bakery in Clear Lake, Iowa, for a cream puff. The right way to eat one was starting at the bottom, where a hint of the cream filling showed the best spot for the first bite. I ate mine in small nibbles until I got to the top. By then, the filling was nearly gone and I popped the last bit of flaky crust into my mouth.

In 1959, I got my first summer job working in the bakery where those sweet delicacies were made. The huge room was hot, teeming with the hum of the ovens, the creak of conveyor belts and the rattle of heavy stainless steel carts as they were wheeled across the floor. I punched a time clock and wore a hairnet, and didn't worry about what I looked like on the job—there were no fellas to get all dolled up for, except for the older man who did the sweeping.

From 7 in the morning, I rolled dough, cut out doughnuts, iced cupcakes, filled jelly rolls and sugared pie crusts. All day long, we loaded and unloaded the ovens.

Our boss, who pushed us to work hard, joined right in on our tasks. She insisted that we take frequent breaks so we wouldn't faint from the heat. She cheerfully admitted that she was plump from "sampling too much of the merchandise," and loved to tease us about our boyfriends and tell us corny jokes that we couldn't help laughing at.

As 3 p.m. approached, I was covered with chocolate icing, strawberry jelly and confectioner's sugar. People stared at my flour-covered face as I left the building at the end of my shift, but I wore my soiled uniform with pride. On the weekends, when I took my sisters to the bakery for a cream puff, I bragged, "I made that!"

A trendy new eating place is going up on the old bakery site now, and high school kids will get summer jobs there. I hope, one day, they will recall their time there as fondly as I remember my days at the town bakery.

LYNDA ANN SCHUMACHER TRAVELERS REST, SC

PIONEERING TEACHER

GRANDMA EDITH BLAZED A TRAIL FOR THE WOMEN IN HER FAMILY.

For 120 years, women in my family have worked full time outside the home while still doing the housekeeping and parenting that needed to be done inside the home. We did it all and loved it.

Grandma Edith Boyd graduated from a New York state teachers training program in 1899. I still have her certificate. She taught third and fourth grades in various schools in the Catskills for 35 years.

Edith was married to a veterinarian who owned a livery stable. She fed not only her family—she had three daughters—but also the dozen male employees of the livery business. She drove her own horse and buggy to the schoolhouse in Corbett, a few miles away, building a fire on the days it was needed.

Grandma never missed a day of work, and she retired in 1934 with a state pension. She came to live with us and continued to help my parents and take care of us kids.

My mom, Marion Dalrymple, attended nurses' training at Carson Peck Memorial Hospital in Brooklyn, New York, where she earned her nursing degree in 1930. She worked at various hospitals—my dad was a New York state trooper and was frequently transferred.

After Dad was injured on the job, Mom found work in a pharmacy; later, during the war, she worked for the Army Air Corps. In 1960, Mom began working at Manatee Memorial Hospital in Bradenton, Florida, and didn't retire fully until she was 75.

I followed in Grandma's footsteps and taught English, starting at Manatee High School in Bradenton in 1967. I married an American history teacher.

My mother-in-law labeled me "a women's libber." I simply thought working was the thing to do: After all, the tradition in my family was for the women to contribute income to the family kitty.

We were proud to do it, and grateful that we could.

SONIA SCHORK TUCSON, AZ

Teacher Edith, top; her daughter Marion, a nurse; and third-generation Sonia, who taught for 35 years.

NIGHTS WITHOUT MOM

THE UNEXPECTED FORCED FAMILY TO MAKE A MAJOR SHIFT.

Our house in Niles, Ohio, was immaculate in the 1940s. Our mom, Mary, who was from Italy, was the embodiment of the stay-at-home wife and mother.

She stretched every dollar by purchasing fabric and sewing our clothes, and buying eggs and poultry at bargain prices while still serving wonderful meals. Through her management, she and our dad, Carmen, who also was born in Italy, were able to meet required costs for our simple lifestyle.

But in 1948 Dad was involved in a car accident. He was uninsured and was found liable for causing damage to three other cars. Soon my parents had insurmountable expenses. I'd heard of people ending up in the poorhouse, and I thought our family was headed there.

Packard Electric in Warren, Ohio, was a successful company that manufactured automotive parts. The mother of the family who lived next door worked there, and Mom confided our troubles to her. She arranged an interview for Mom, and to our surprise and delight, our stay-at-home mom was hired to work on one of the auto parts lines.

By the fall of 1948, our family had a new routine to accommodate Mom's second-shift schedule. She got us ready for school and made supper so Dad could heat it up when he got home from his job at Stevens Metal Products in Niles. My brother, named Carmen after Dad, was 7. I was 9. Sis Theresa, 12, was our supervisor.

On winter evenings, Sis popped corn for us and made Hershey's hot cocoa as Mom had done. In the summer evenings, Dad would make a fire outside and let us roast wieners and marshmallows. We'd play until dusk, when his whistle called us home.

We couldn't avoid some mishaps without Mom. I once burned a hole in a new nylon dress as I was ironing it, and another time, I accidentally put a slit in a tablecloth while working on a science project.

We also got away with things that Mom might have prevented. I found and opened

Happily stay-at-home until she had to find a job, Mary was resilient and kept her family on an even keel.

the Christmas presents that Mom had hidden under my parents' bed, although I tried to rewrap them. Once I ate an entire bunch of bananas. Another time, I practiced my cooking skills by frying sunny-side up eggs. So much for Sis' supervision!

By 1951, we were used to managing without Mom. We still missed her presence at school events and wished for her during emergencies, but our improvising had paid off. Mom handed over her paychecks, keeping only $20 for herself, until my parents were debt-free; after that, she kept all but $20 for herself. She modernized to fit in with her co-workers, painting her nails and perming her hair.

Those nights without Mom required cooperation from every family member, but Mom gets the credit for the biggest transformation. Our secluded, demure mother showed great courage and an ability to adapt when she entered the workforce, and emerged as the savior of our family.

ANNETTE KOCHERA BROOKFIELD, OH

★ Joyce worked a desk job at the telephone company from 1951 to 1954.

FRESH FACE AT MA BELL

WHILE MY HUSBAND, DICK, was in the Air Force during the Korean War, I found work as a repair and installation clerk at Southwestern Bell Telephone Co. in San Antonio, Texas, where he'd been sent for basic training.

Dick and I were newly married, and he worked in the administration building, known as the Taj Mahal, at Randolph Field. From my observation, the main office where he worked was supposed to be staffed with tall, handsome men, and Dick fit the bill.

We eventually returned home to Rockford, Illinois, where we had three daughters. We've been married for more than 70 years. Who could ask for more?

JOYCE WHITTINGTON PECATONICA, IL

QUALITY ON-THE-JOB TRAINING

HE LEARNED THE REWARDS OF LOYALTY.

The clerk who answered the phone at Erickson's Quality Store in Viola, Illinois, always stretched out the name: "Quaaaality." This impressed on callers that they'd reached the store that sold only high-quality items, such as the Del Monte, Monarch and Libby's canned goods that were difficult to get during World War II.

Mr. Erickson was a terrific salesman. Shoppers rarely turned him down when he suggested they "really should try" something. The customer was king—or queen, mostly. Besides Mr. Erickson and me, his wife, Dorothy, and Loretta Esp waited on customers. Shoppers read their lists to us and we gathered items one at a time. No supermarket efficiency for us!

Although wartime shortages were a constant theme, most people didn't complain, knowing soldiers had it so much worse. Our shelves were partly empty at times, but no one went away empty-handed. We made sure our loyal customers were taken care of even when items were scarce. I was only 13, yet I learned to tell white lies. With a straight face, I'd tell a shopper, "No, we don't have any black pepper," adding to myself, "for you, because you're not a regular customer."

But for a regular, Loretta would whisper, "Put three bananas in a sack for her." She often told me, "If you do this for me, I'll dance at your wedding."

My main job was stocking shelves, but I could do every job in the store except cut steak. My least favorite job was cleaning the meat display cabinet. I had to climb inside with a bucket of hot, soapy water. I was sure I looked silly inside the cabinet.

Beef was in very short supply during those war years, and so Mr. Erickson developed a system. It started with an order of canned goods from Herman Gremmel in Muscatine, Iowa. Since Mr. Erickson was a good customer, Mr. Gremmel also let him have a case of cigarettes. The cigarettes were rationed out to our regulars (two packs a week), but Mr. Erickson also used a few cartons to close the deal on a side of beef—obtained from a mysterious supplier in Davenport, Iowa. He'd spend much of Friday night cutting and wrapping the meat orders, which he would mark with a family name and the amount owed.

I worked at Erickson's from eighth grade until I graduated from high school. The experience helped me get hired at IBM after I graduated from college.

CHARLES R. SCHAECHTER MOLINE, IL

WONDER DRUGS

When aches and fevers delay work, there's nothing as simple as "take two and call me in the morning"!

Feelin' No Pain

In 1960, Bristol-Myers introduced Excedrin, with more ingredients providing more relief for more symptoms. It may have seemed as potent as a tranquilizer, but the combo drug contained nothing new— just aspirin, acetaminophen and caffeine.

THE EXTRA-STRENGTH PAIN RELIEVER

Tablet for tablet, Excedrin® is *50% stronger than aspirin* for relief of headache pain.

New Excedrin gives you 1) a fast-acting pain reliever 2) a long-lasting pain reliever 3) a tension reliever to relax you 4) an anti-depressant to restore your spirits.

Excedrin contains more kinds and more quantity of ingredients than any other leading pain tablet. Yet Excedrin is safe enough that you need no prescription.

To relieve pain of headache, sinus, cramps, even temporary relief of minor arthritic pain—ask for Excedrin (pronounced: ek-SEDD-rin), the extra-strength pain reliever.

NEW FROM BRISTOL-MYERS

'62

HEADACHE·SINUS·CRAMPS·ARTHRITIS

Excedrin
EXTRA-STRENGTH PAIN RELIEVER
HEADACHE · ARTHRITIS
SINUSITIS · COLDS · TOOTHACHE
MENSTRUAL PAIN

Excedrin® Excedrin
EXTRA-STRENGTH PAIN RELIEVER
SYMPTOMATIC RELIEF FOR PAIN OF
HEADACHE · ARTHRITIS · SINUSITIS · COLDS · TOOTHACHE

For Colds and Flu...

DOCTORS RECOMMEND:

1. Rest in bed
2. Drink plenty of fluids
3. Take aspirin to reduce fever and relieve pain

Reporting on a Government-Financed Study of Five Leading Pain Relievers, an article in The Journal of The American Medical Association shows that Bayer Aspirin is as gentle to the stomach as any product tested, including the higher priced buffered product. Furthermore, not even the higher priced combination-of-ingredients one that claims to be 50% stronger nor any of these products is faster or stronger than Bayer Aspirin.

'65

BAYER ASPIRIN
FAST PAIN RELIEF

BAYER ASPIRIN FOR CHILDREN

Time-Tested

Well before this ad ran, aspirin had lost ground to upstart pain relievers like Tylenol. But Bayer had history on its side: A proven fever reducer, Bayer reminded flu victims that aspirin still had their backs.

ONE GOOD TURN

A SPLIT-SECOND DECISION ON THE RIDE HOME SET HER LIFE ON A NEW COURSE.

Palm Sunday, 1972: My wife, Barbara, our three children and I were on our way home from church when we happened to pass by the base for our local volunteer emergency service.

"Stop the car!" Barbara said. "I want to join the ambulance corps."

I immediately turned into the parking lot and Barbara went in to pick up a membership application. So began my wife's 35-year career as a volunteer first responder.

She started with training to be a dispatcher, which included basic first aid. To say that the emergency medical bug bit her from that point would be putting it mildly. She went from dispatcher to first medic in a very short time. Her early training included advanced first aid and CPR. That was followed by an emergency medical technician course.

Over the years, she became an expert at teaching others emergency skills. She trained dispatchers, medics and drivers; then she became director of training. At one point, she had trained more than 50% of the active ambulance corps membership as EMTs.

But she didn't stop there. She went on to become a critical care technician and then a certified paramedic. This training, along with her studies and her experiences in the field, made her a valuable and highly sought after instructor in emergency medical techniques.

For many years, Barbara taught courses throughout New York's Monroe County and adjacent counties, including a stint teaching critical care as an adjunct professor at a local community college.

Thirty-five years dedicated to saving lives and teaching others how to save lives. Not bad for someone who was just driving by a parking lot one long-ago Sunday in March.

DAVID ACKROYD FAIRPORT, NY

Barbara Ackroyd enjoys a coffee with fellow ambulance corps member Roger Boas during a rare lull between calls.

Driving an ambulance in Waco, Texas, wasn't enough to prepare Neal (right) for a wild trip behind a speedy sheriff's deputy.

HECK OF A RIDE

DRIVING AN AMBULANCE, SOMETIMES ONE NEEDS A LITTLE HELP.

During the summer of 1956, I worked for the Wyman Roberts Funeral Home in my hometown in Texas. In those days, funeral homes provided ambulance service—and that was one of my duties at Wyman Roberts (along with driving the hearse). I had some experience with emergency response: While at Baylor University the previous spring, I'd worked for the A-1 Ambulance service in Waco.

The funeral home's ambulance was a 1956 Pontiac with a cot, two red lights mounted on the grille, and a siren. It couldn't match today's emergency vehicles, but we made do.

One Sunday afternoon, a two-car crash on U.S. Route 96 left two women badly hurt. Their injuries were so severe they had to be transferred for treatment to Houston, about three hours away.

We loaded the patients into the back of the Pontiac and a nurse settled next to them on a stool to monitor their condition.

I'd worked out my route—Jasper, Woodville, Livingston, Cleveland, Houston—but I was nervous about getting there quickly without endangering the patients. My heart leapt every time we went through a red light at an intersection.

As we neared Houston, freeway drivers weren't pulling over for my siren, so I called the Harris County sheriff from a pay phone, asking for an escort.

I soon spotted the patrol car ahead of me, and the race was on. He sped off, driving much faster than I wanted to go, but since I had no clue where the hospital was, I had no choice but to stay right with him.

The deputy was charging down Fannin Street in busy downtown Houston, hopping lanes, dodging vehicles and even nudging the curb at one point. And I was repeating every hop, dodge and nudge. When the hospital finally came into view, I breathed a sigh of relief.

We got the patients safely inside and I went over to shake the deputy's hand.

"That was a heck of a ride," I told him.

He laughed. "All in a day's work."

NEAL MURPHY SAN AUGUSTINE, TX

> ## AS WE NEARED HOUSTON, FREEWAY DRIVERS WEREN'T PULLING OVER FOR MY SIREN.
> ★

BORN INTO THE BUSINESS

In small towns like Harper, Kansas, it isn't unusual to have second- and third-generation volunteer firefighters. But that makes us no less proud. Two of the Ummel grandchildren, Jaci and her brother Garrison, serve as volunteers, along with their father, my son Gary, who is a 25-year veteran of the Harper Fire Department.

SHIRLEY UMMEL HARPER, KS

★ ★ ★

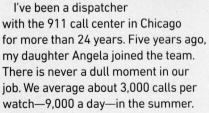

JUST LIKE MOM

We represent those who are rarely seen—the calm voice in the dark, the link holding it all together.

I've been a dispatcher with the 911 call center in Chicago for more than 24 years. Five years ago, my daughter Angela joined the team. There is never a dull moment in our job. We average about 3,000 calls per watch—9,000 a day—in the summer.

We are proud of our work, helping the police to serve and protect the citizens of our city.

SHARON PLOSKI CHICAGO, IL

HER FIRST BATTLE WAS THE TOUGHEST

WHEN AN AMBULANCE COMPANY relocated to a different town, leaving our upstate New York community with the nearest service 20 minutes away, I decided to train as an EMT. I was 40 years old at the time. I joined a group of new fire department recruits for first responder training. I was delighted when I passed the course but disappointed to learn I couldn't use my new skills without being attached to a fire department or ambulance service.

So I looked into becoming a firefighter. This was the mid-1970s and I didn't know any women who were firefighters. On the other hand, since I'd already trained with some of the members, I didn't think I'd have a problem getting in. But when I asked a friend to sponsor me, he said no.

"We do not have or want women in the department," he told me.

I went to the fire chief—and he said no, too. Finally, after four weeks of trying to find a way in, I wrote to the president of the firemen's association to say I'd decided against joining the department. His reaction surprised me.

"Rita, stick to your guns and I'll help you," he said.

He called for a union vote—and the membership voted in my favor. After that, I had a lot of support, especially because I went through the tough training to fight fires.

I was with that fire department for 20 years. In 1997, I won the award for firefighter of the year.

Sometimes being the first is a little scary, but God puts us where he wants us. I'm in my 80s now and still very proud of having been a firefighter.

RITA WAGNER VERNON CENTER, NY

Rita's award for firefighter of the year has the inscription "for unselfish service and dedication."

★ One can still find spots like the Boulevard Diner in Worcester, Massachusetts, for comfort food.

MEMORIES OF BIG MIKE

THE HIGHWAY DINER in Babylon Village, Long Island, New York, was the typical 24-hour diner in the 1960s and '70s. The coffee was always hot, the burgers were the best in the village, and it was the final stop before heading home. Big Mike was the owner and made most of the food cooked there.

During senior year in high school, we got coffee before walking to school. At lunchtime, we made the two-block trek to get a good greasy burger, a bag of fries and a drink for two bucks.

When we went out on dates, the Highway was the last call for a good cup of coffee and something sweet from the bakery counter.

After high school, I volunteered at the local firehouse, a block away from the diner. After fire calls, the Highway once again was the place to go. Big Mike would make faces when 25 or more of us came in all at once and ordered burgers. When the fire horns went off, we'd all run out, leaving the food on the counters and tables.

Mike would holler at us in Greek for leaving, but he knew we'd come back to pay the bills. Most of the time, when we came back after the call, he would start all over, making fresh burgers and fries and charging only for the first order.

When Big Mike died, the Highway became a thing of the past. It's hard to explain to today's youngsters the impact that place had on us.

GUY SCHNEIDER MILLER PLACE, NY

PICTURES FROM THE PAST
★★★ Heartland ★★★

NEWEST FARMHAND

This photo of grandfather and grandson, hand in hand around 1966, has special significance for me. My dad, Jonath F. Graber, with whom I farmed, decided to go check on the cattle or take care of a chore. My son Kendall, about age 2, took Grandpa's hand and walked out with him on his errand. I was born in 1928 and have many wonderful memories of growing up on the family farm.

LEO GRABER MARION, SD

FIELD WORK

My dad, Jim Dailey, is shown here in the mid-1940s after he returned from World War II. Dad was just outside of Sweetwater, Tennessee, taking a wagonload of tobacco to the barn to be cured. He worked very hard all his life and was well respected by all who knew him.

FLOYD DAILEY CLEVELAND, OH

FORGING A CAREER

Blacksmith work, a business of the past, was very necessary to a farming community. The man pictured in this 1950s photo is my father, Tom Dolezal, who owned and operated a blacksmith shop for 36 years in the little town of Shiner.

EDWIN DOLEZAL NEW BRAUNFELS, TX

NO MATTER THE WEATHER

In 1966, I took this photo of my daughter Rhonda, 9, and her cousin-in-law Warren Osthoff, flexing his muscles after stacking 2,500 straw bales for grass seeding along I-270 in Missouri. Temperatures climbed as high as 107 degrees that day.

ROBERTA NADLER AUGUSTA, MO

The lesson of neighborly kindness Lloyd saw growing up near Meriden, KS, stuck with him.

FRIENDLY HANDS MAKE LIGHT WORK

ACCIDENT AT HARVESTTIME BROUGHT FARM NEIGHBORS TOGETHER.

Helping neighbors was something everyone did when I was growing up on a farm near Meriden, Kansas, in the '40s and '50s.

Near the end of one wheat season, our neighbor Raymond had a terrible accident. My dad, Laoel, and I kept an eye on his crop, and one day we decided it was ready and started up our 1941 Farmall H tractor and pull type combine, an Allis-Chalmers All-Crop 66. We knew that when the neighbors saw us harvesting Raymond's field, they would come and help if they could.

Sure enough, after we started cutting, people began to show up with equipment: more combines, balers, trucks, and tractors with plows and disks. The wheat field was about 25 acres, pretty big for eastern Kansas at that time. The combines were small—ours cut a 5½-foot swath; the ones today can cut a swath 60 feet wide. A combine that big couldn't even have turned around in the field.

By midafternoon, the farmers' wives, mothers and other family members began to arrive, bringing fried chicken, pies and more for the army of workers. At the end of the day, Raymond's wheat had been harvested and taken to the elevator; the straw was cut, baled and stored; and the field was plowed and reworked. Raymond was able to come out of the house and watch all the activity from his yard. He knew that everyone had their own farms to take care of and what it meant that his neighbors had spent their day helping.

Farmers like to brag a little about how much better their tractors are than someone else's—it's all in fun—but most of the talk that day was about how fast Raymond's crop went from a field of wheat to one ready for the next crop.

Several years ago I moved to an over-55 community, where we still try to help one another. The appreciation for neighbors helping neighbors has stayed with me my entire life.

LLOYD RICHARDS MOORESVILLE, NC

★★★ A FRESH VIEW ★★★

My husband, Verdell, was a photographer and aviation expert. He took this picture of a farmer studying an aerial shot of his property in the 1940s.

DOROTHY HALLINGSTAD SPARTA, WI

THEY LEFT THEIR MARK

Presidents, astronauts, artists, musicians and other notable figures made a lasting impact on our nation's culture.

Apollo 11 astronauts Michael Collins, Neil Armstrong and Edwin "Buzz" Aldrin in front of the lunar landing module simulator in 1969; President John F. Kennedy fields questions at a press conference in 1963; and, below, Buddy Holly and the Crickets on the BBC TV show *Off the Record*.

Burton, at right in 1964, was glad to meet President Harry Truman, above, in 1953 and get his autograph. ★

SPENDING TIME WITH TRUMAN

CHANCE ENCOUNTER WITH THE FORMER PRESIDENT OF THE UNITED STATES MADE A STRONG IMPRESSION ON KIDS AND ADULTS ALIKE.

I took my seventh grade class from William Cullen Bryant Elementary School, in Kansas City, Missouri, on a field trip in April 1953. We traveled by train to the state Capitol, in Jefferson City, but the highlight occurred on the way home.

One of the chaperones, Mrs. Oliver, informed me that former President Harry S. Truman was aboard the train in one of the forward staterooms, and he had agreed to come back to our car and visit with the students.

Mrs. Oliver and I sat in the front seat of the car, awaiting his arrival. Ten minutes later, I looked up, and there stood the man who just three months earlier had been the leader of the free world.

There were no military bands playing, no Secret Service agents attending and no politicians tagging behind. A small man in a double-breasted suit and thick eyeglasses stood there with a big grin across his face.

After introductions, Mrs. Oliver left the two of us sitting together in the front seat while she hurried to the next car to bring other chaperones to meet Mr. Truman.

I felt rather tongue-tied. What could I say to the man who had conferred with world leaders like Roosevelt, Churchill, Stalin, Eisenhower, the pope and many others?

Knowing that there were thirty 12-year-olds behind us trying to hear what we were saying didn't help, either!

Mr. Truman soon put me at ease, chatting and asking me about my students, family and service in the Navy.

After the other chaperones were introduced, the president made his way down the aisle and greeted each student with a handshake, a few pleasant words and a big smile. Then he waited patiently while every student with a camera had their picture taken shaking hands with him. He never once lost his big grin.

After he left the car, I began tearing off sheets of the Missouri Pacific Railroad notepad Mr. Truman had handed me minutes earlier. He had taken the time to sign his autograph on each of the 40 sheets in the pad. So I passed out one to every student and chaperone. And I have that small scrap of paper to this day.

As the train pulled into the station at Independence, where the Trumans lived, it was raining and nearly dark. The kids opened the windows (Missouri Pacific still used such windows back then) and poked their heads out, hoping to get one more glimpse of Mr. Truman as he left the train.

No one was there to meet him or carry his luggage. We saw him step down from the train, put on his big brown felt hat, grab his luggage and take a detour toward our car, where 30 children and their chaperones were cheering and yelling goodbyes.

He stopped near our train car, put down his luggage, removed his hat and stood there in the drizzling rain, waving to our group.

Of those 30 youngsters, I'll bet not one of them has ever forgotten our meeting with the man in the double-breasted suit and big felt hat.

BURTON HALE SAN DIEGO, CA

Delighted with her letter from first lady Mamie Eisenhower, Diane posed with her mom, Lois, for a photo that ran in a local newspaper. ★

SHE LIKED IKE—AND MAMIE TOO

HER PORTRAITS OF THE PRESIDENT AND FIRST LADY GET A SURPRISING AND CHERISHED RESPONSE.

Back in 1956, my parents watched politics on TV often. Even though there were just three commercial stations and a public television station (WTTW, "Window to the World") in the Chicago area, they managed to cover President Dwight D. Eisenhower well. Not only was he our president, he was running for reelection that fall.

It was perfectly normal to see my father, Art Henrikson, sketching caricatures of Ike and other politicians while watching television. After all, he made a living drawing gag and editorial cartoons for local newspapers.

In June 1956, my dad even created an animated character for WNBQ-TV to introduce color television to Chicagoland. Red-haired Tommy Tint was dressed in a green shirt and blue overalls. Tommy painted the town and blew it up with a dynamite plunger to show off the vivid primary colors and entice the audience to tune in. Unfortunately, our family did not own a color TV set, so we missed seeing Tommy and WNBQ in living color.

As an enthusiastic preschooler, I positioned my own small desk and chair in front of our black-and-white TV set during the evening news. I loved Ike. My parents wore "I Like Ike" campaign buttons, and my grandmother even wore a rhinestone IKE pin to promote his reelection.

Soon I started imitating my dad and drew and colored my own caricatures of Ike. I eventually added first lady Mamie to my repertoire. I especially loved her bangs and red hat.

My dad was not shy about his pride in my drawings of Ike and Mamie. He also was a loyal Republican. Ironically, the Democratic presidential candidate that election was Adlai Stevenson, who was from our home state of Illinois.

One day, my dad suggested that I mail my drawings of Ike and Mamie to the president and first lady. I carefully drew and colored special drawings for each of them. My mom, Lois, addressed the envelope to the White House, placed my drawings inside and drove them to the nearest post office.

I continued doing the normal things a 4-year-old does: attending preschool and Sunday school, playing with my neighborhood friends and singing along with the albums of my favorite musicals.

Two weeks after the November election, my parents brought in the mail and exclaimed, "You have a letter from the White House, Diane!"

They carefully opened the envelope. Inside, on White House stationery, was a letter signed by the first lady. My mom read it aloud:

> Dear Diane,
> I do want to thank you ever so much for the wonderful pictures you drew of the President and me. Our hearts were truly touched when we received them, and I assure you we are both more than delighted to have them as a special token of your sincere friendship.
> With gratitude and very best wishes to you and your family,
> Mamie Doud Eisenhower

I was thrilled beyond words. I screamed with excitement as any 4-year-old would. I told all of my friends, while my parents called and wrote our relatives.

My parents took it one step further. They contacted several Chicago and Des Plaines local newspapers. Shortly afterward, reporters and a photographer came to our house to interview us and take a photo of my mother and me with the letter. The newspaper articles were published in late November 1956.

I became an even bigger fan of Ike and Mamie, of course. My parents mailed my valentine to them in early 1958. I was surprised to receive a second letter from the White House. It was written on White House letterhead and signed by the first lady's secretary.

My treasured 1956 letter from first lady Mamie Eisenhower hangs on my wall to this day. And I still like Ike...and Mamie.

DIANE HENRIKSON RUSSELL BRANDON, FL

COFFEE BREAK WITH RONALD REAGAN

BEHIND THE SCENES AT THE ROSE BOWL PARADE.

M y wife, Josephine, and I attended the Rose Parade in Pasadena, California, in 1959. We arrived early in the morning, parked at the stadium and walked a mile back to the parade route. We found a curbside spot on Orange Grove Boulevard, in the second block down from where the parade makes the turn onto Colorado Boulevard. We set up our folding chairs to await the start of the parade.

Josephine wanted a cup of coffee, so I volunteered to walk up the street and find a place to buy two cups. A policeman was directing foot traffic, and as I asked him where to find a coffee stand, a panel truck drove up behind the grandstand. "Watch where the driver of the truck sets up—he will be selling coffee and pastries," the officer said.

Behind the massive grandstand, sure enough, the driver had set up a table with doughnuts and coffee urns. I poured myself some coffee and, as I looked around for someone to pay, I found myself staring across the table into the face of Ronald Reagan.

Gathered around him were his wife, Nancy; Audrey Meadows of *The Jackie Gleason Show*; and legendary sports announcer Mel Allen. Reagan was the TV host for the event, and Meadows and Allen were providing commentary.

No one said a word to me as I stood there; I may have looked like part of the crew that was working the coffee truck. I overheard their conversation, which was about grass fires in the Santa Monica area the night before.

Then a parade organizer told the group it was time for the event to start, and that they were to take the elevator to the top of the grandstand.

Nancy said, "Ronnie, I'm going to miss you." Reagan pointed at the platform and said, "I'll only be right up there, honey."

I gathered up my coffee and doughnuts and went back to tell my story to Josephine. Of course, she didn't believe me.

WALT BORLA SANDY, UT

In Reagan's career as an actor, he traveled around the country as a spokesman for CBS' popular *General Electric Theater* series from 1954 to '62.

SURPRISE ARRIVAL AT THE WHITE HOUSE

INSIDER TOUR ENDS WITH MEETING PRESIDENT JIMMY CARTER.

My first time on an airplane was to visit my cousins, the Dudleys, in Cheverly, Maryland, in 1979.

Cousin Ed, as I called the father of my cousins Karen-Ann and Terry, worked at the communications center inside the White House, and was authorized to take us on a private tour.

Ed was on a first-name basis with everyone we met walking down the long hallways. We'd just exited the Oval Office when someone pulled Ed aside to tell him the president was arriving. "Let's go," Ed said.

We hustled onto the White House lawn, where brass stanchions and crimson ropes corralled the gathering crowd. Men in suits and dark glasses, holding walkie-talkies, ran onto the lawn. We covered our ears and squinted as a helicopter landed on the carpet of green. Then

> WE'D JUST EXITED THE OVAL OFFICE WHEN SOMEONE PULLED ED ASIDE TO TELL HIM THE PRESIDENT WAS ARRIVING.
>
> ★

the door opened and the 39th president of the United States, Jimmy Carter, stepped out.

First lady Rosalynn Carter joined him from inside the White House and together they greeted the people who'd gathered on the lawn. I took photos with my little camera. Ed pushed us tightly against the silk ropes so we could shake hands with the president and first lady.

My photos turned out grainy, but about a week after I got home, I received a color photo of me shaking hands with President Carter. Ed had tracked down one of the official photographers from that day to get the picture for me.

I'll always be grateful to my dear Cousin Ed for making the first of my many life's adventures one of the most memorable.

LAURIE BRENNEKE-ROLLINS ACUSHNET, MA

Kevin showed an early interest in politics, thanks to his parents, Anna and Edwin.

LUCKY FIND ON THE CAMPAIGN TRAIL

HUBERT HUMPHREY'S LOSS (OF A TIE CLIP) WAS A WIN FOR ONE CONSTITUENT.

During the hotly contested 1968 presidential election, Vice President Hubert Humphrey, who was the Democratic presidential nominee, made two trips to the Lehigh Valley in Pennsylvania. The valley is a large population center that includes Allentown, Bethlehem, Easton and many surrounding communities, and with unionized companies like Bethlehem Steel and Mack Trucks, it was vital to Humphrey's campaign.

In the usual bustle at the airport, there were a lot of people around Humphrey as he made his way to a waiting car. He gave his speech and returned to the airport to go on to the next stop.

The next morning my father, Edwin, who worked at an Allentown engineering firm, was at the airport to pick up some business associates when something shiny lying by the curb caught his eye. Amazingly, it was Humphrey's tie clasp, which he lost in the jostling the day before.

My father was definitely a Richard Nixon supporter and even though I was only 8, I remember staying up late with my parents the night of that election, watching the results trickle in. We all fell asleep after midnight and woke to find Nixon had won. I was probably one of the few fourth graders watching those returns. But it was a sign of things to come because I still love politics.

And more than 50 years later, I still have Humphrey's tie clip.

> ## AT THE AIRPORT, THERE WERE A LOT OF PEOPLE AROUND HUMPHREY AS HE MADE HIS WAY TO A WAITING CAR.
> ★

KEVIN BRADLEY NORTHAMPTON, PA

FLASH JUDGMENT

YOUNG REPORTER WAS CROWDED OUT OF MEETING JFK.

When I was in seventh grade, I was assistant editor of our school paper in Lebanon, Oregon, the *Crowfoot Flash*. In the spring of 1960, the students who worked on the monthly paper went to the state Capitol in Salem to interview Gov. Mark Hatfield.

While I waited nervously for our appointment, a well-dressed man came into the Capitol rotunda. A group of women rushed to gather around him. I figured he must be important, so I joined the crowd to get his autograph on my notepad. But try as I might, every time I put my pad out for him to sign, someone else would put theirs on top of it. Frustrated, I gave up. Later, I heard he was a senator from Massachusetts, so I figured he didn't matter to me anyway.

Several weeks went by before, one evening, I saw the same man on TV. It was John F. Kennedy, and he had been in Oregon stumping for president of the United States. If I had known then what I knew later, nothing could have stopped me from getting that autograph.

JOHN E. LEARD LEBANON, OR

LATER, I HEARD HE WAS A SENATOR FROM MASSACHUSETTS, SO I FIGURED HE DIDN'T MATTER TO ME ANYWAY.

★

John F. Kennedy's strategic campaign to key states won over party leaders and voters.

FDR'S 1936 landslide victory over Republican challenger Alfred M. Landon remains the most lopsided win in Electoral College history. He won 523 votes, losing only Maine's five and Vermont's three. ★

AMUSING FDR

My grandfather James A. "Pop" Murray passionately cherished his right to vote and voted in every election for which he was eligible. He cast his first vote for presidential candidate William Jennings Bryan, describing him as the best orator he'd ever heard.

Pop was a registered Democrat, but he would vote for candidates of both parties, saying that people should vote for the person, not the party. He attended the inaugurations of six presidents: William H. Taft, Herbert Hoover, Woodrow Wilson, Theodore Roosevelt, Franklin D. Roosevelt and Dwight Eisenhower.

The year FDR won 46 out of 48 states (1936), Pop wrote to the White House suggesting Mr. Roosevelt demand a recount in those two states. Roosevelt's secretary wrote back to say the president had had a real laugh over the letter.

KEN RASHEFF LAWRENCEVILLE, GA

SO NEAR AND NOW SO FAR

BACK IN 1960, I was going to school in Chicago and had a part-time job with a catering company. On Sept. 26, 1960, I was working the banquet where Sen. John F. Kennedy was to speak after his first debate with Vice President Richard M. Nixon. The banquet was a full sit-down dinner, and it was packed.

As both a Republican and a Protestant, I was not a Kennedy fan. Indeed, I'm sorry to say that I was quite the opposite.

So I don't know why I pushed to get to the front of the greeters when Kennedy arrived. But there I was in line to shake his hand. He was moving closer, and I was determined not to shake his hand or even to look into his face. I recall this decision with great regret today. I do remember the questions he asked the waitresses standing on either side of me: "Is everyone well in your family? Does your husband have a steady job? Do you feel your children are getting a good education?" He was so personable, I wondered at the time if he actually knew them.

Later that evening, he gave a speech that seemed to hypnotize his audience. Cheers, laughter, silence—whatever the senator wanted from the crowd, he got.

Oh, how neat it would have been for me—a future teacher of American history—to be able to say that I had met and shaken hands with John Kennedy. But I can't.

I did learn a valuable lesson, though: Don't allow personal prejudice to keep you from doing something you may regret. *Carpe diem!*

BOB McILHENNY SAN DIEGO, CA

On the campaign trail in October 1960, enthusiastic supporters applaud Kennedy's arrival in Columbus, OH. ★

SKIP THE FORMALITIES

ELEANOR ROOSEVELT PREFERRED BEING WITH THOSE WHO HAPPENED BY.

Working on Ohio University's administrative staff in the spring of 1954, I was assigned to meet former first lady Eleanor Roosevelt at the Columbus airport. Accompanied by Richard Bitters, director of press relations, we were to drive her to the swanky University Club in Columbus for lunch before escorting her 75 miles south to the Athens campus.

When Mrs. Roosevelt was a delegate to the U.N. General Assembly, our university President John C. Baker served as the first chief American representative to UNESCO. Like many others, Dr. Baker was greatly moved by her efforts as head of the Human Rights Commission.

Their friendship enabled him to convince the woman that he considered one of the world's greatest humanitarians to give a speech at the central auditorium of Ohio's oldest university. The speech would be broadcast on public radio.

All went well until Mrs. Roosevelt got off the plane. When Dick and I explained the lunch arrangements, she politely protested. Instead of a fancy luncheon, she preferred "to have lunch

> OVER THE YEARS, WHERE WE ATE HAS FADED, BUT THE EXPERIENCE WAS UNFORGETTABLE.
>
> ★

among folks who just happen to come by. Do you know of a fast-food place?"

We called our president, who answered right away. Dick launched into a rapid-fire explanation about why Mrs. Roosevelt would miss out on meeting with state dignitaries.

Baker broke in. "Whoa, Dick. Before you and Dave share heart attacks, let me explain." The lunch, he told us, was part of a regularly scheduled Ohio College Presidents Association meeting, and everyone would understand. "She truly is a person of the people," Baker said. "So take good care of her."

Over the years, where we ate has faded, but the experience was unforgettable. Sitting at a corner booth, whenever someone approached, Mrs. Roosevelt would smile and say, "Yes, I'm Eleanor Roosevelt, and what is your name?" Then she exchanged a friendly greeting before asking questions about their lives.

Somehow we managed to finish our meal. Eleanor Roosevelt may have had her detractors, but I can guarantee there weren't any in that restaurant on April 26, 1954.

DAVID NEAL KELLER DUBLIN, OH

PICTURES FROM THE PAST
★★★ May the Best ★★★
Candidate Win

QUICK TOUCH-UP
My husband, Kenneth, is seen here fixing election decorations on our family car before a campaign stop in Lebanon by Republican presidential candidate Barry Goldwater in October 1964.
WINIFRED PUSHOR LEBANON, IN

SHOWING SUPPORT
This young woman's sign shows that the voting age was 21 in 1964. Presidential candidate Barry Goldwater carried the Hoosier State in the GOP primaries.
WINIFRED PUSHOR LEBANON, IN

COMIC RELIEF
In 1968, my family would gather on Sunday nights to watch our favorite TV show, *The Smothers Brothers Comedy Hour*.

My favorite comedy bit was the faux presidential campaign of Pat Paulsen, who ran for his Straight Talking American Government (STAG) party.

I bought this Pat Paulsen for President button back in 1968, and I've pulled it out for every presidential election since. It always brings back pleasant memories and laughs. It's surprising how many people remember that campaign.
DAVID SEIBEL ROSEBURG, OR

IN A NEW HOME

After winning the governor's race on Nov. 8, 1966, Ronald Reagan toured the executive mansion in Sacramento, CA, on New Year's Day 1967 with his wife, Nancy, and children Patricia, 14, and Ronald Jr., 8. Three months later, the family moved out for safety reasons.

WALKING ON AIR

WHEN THE LUNAR LANDER REACHED THE MOON with Neil Armstrong and Buzz Aldrin aboard in 1969, I was in Vietnam with the 65th Engineer Battalion, which was attached to the 25th Infantry Division at the Army base in Cu Chi.

I was about to start my shift on guard duty in the motor pool. Not wanting to miss the milestone of the first man on the moon, I'd slipped my transistor radio into my uniform pocket just before my shift.

Transistor radios weren't allowed on guard duty, so I hid under a truck to keep an eye out for the sergeant while I tuned in to the broadcast.

I'll never forget the excitement of listening to the moon landing while lying under that truck. The surge of patriotism and pride running through me was wonderful. I was lucky that the guard sergeant didn't make his rounds then, because I was so caught up in what I was hearing that I probably wouldn't have noticed him.

The experience remains my best memory from my time as a combat engineer in Vietnam—and one of the best of my life.

Succeeding generations may never fully appreciate how momentous the moon landing was at the time

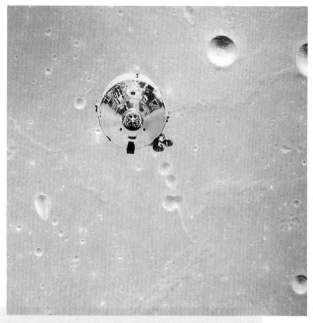

The command and service modules in lunar orbit with Michael Collins on board, as seen from the lunar lander on its descent orbit. ★

and continues to be for my generation. Having lived through so many tragic events for America since then, from school shootings to terror attacks, we cherish the positive memory of that historic moment.

GARY PEDIGO BRIGHTON, CO

A DAY OF CELEBRATION

New Yorkers give an exuberant welcome to Apollo 11 astronauts Buzz Aldrin, Michael Collins and Neil Armstrong with a ticker tape parade on Aug. 13, 1969.

★ Neil Armstrong (center) and Buzz Aldrin (right) are seen standing near their lunar module in this reproduction taken from a telecast by the Apollo 11 lunar surface camera.

THEIR HEARTS WERE IN IT

THE DUTY ROSTER WAS POSTED, and my heart sank. I worked in coronary care at Mercy Hospital in Mason City, Iowa, and was scheduled for the evening shift on July 20, 1969—the planned date of the first moonwalk.

Perhaps it's hard to believe now how much excitement we all felt about seeing what was on the moon. But at the time, no one would have missed it for the world.

Our coronary unit consisted of four rooms, each opening onto a central desk area, and was staffed with two nurses. We were only half full that night, and the two patients were as eager as we were to see the event.

We didn't know the exact time of the walk, but our anticipation was palpable. Instead of staying at the desk, the other nurse and I each took a patient and sat next to their beds, alternating between watching the heart monitors and the TVs. We all talked enthusiastically to each other from the rooms, the four of us united like a family sharing this unforgettable moment. We cheered together when Neil Armstrong touched the surface of the moon.

When it was over, each patient had a souvenir of the occasion—an EKG strip showing his heart rhythm at the exact moment of the moon landing. I'm happy to say normal sinus rhythm prevailed through all the excitement.

JUDY JONES WICHITA, KS

Fifteen minutes after stepping onto the moon, Neil Armstrong captures Buzz Aldrin's descent down the module ladder in a series of photographs. ★

BRAVISSIMO!

In 1969, I was an airman stationed in the heel of Italy, living with my wife and baby daughters in a small apartment 20 miles from the base. We couldn't afford a TV, but there were no English language stations anyway. When Apollo 11 was about to land, the few Italians who did own sets brought them out to the sidewalk so anyone could watch.

It was a thrill for me to hear everything in English before the Italian translation. But you could feel everyone's pride as we watched together.

DUANE E. LYON OAKWOOD, GA

THE NEXT GENERATION

FORTY YEARS AFTER THE ASTRONAUTS first walked on the moon, I was in Florida to see the launch of the space shuttle *Endeavor*. My daughter Dawn's husband, Tim Kopra, was aboard.

Tim lived on the International Space Station for two months in 2009, and then returned for six months in 2015 as the Expedition 47 commander. In all, Tim has spent 244 days in space. This is a picture of him (below) on one of his three spacewalks.

Sitting in front of the TV in 1969, holding baby Dawn, I waited for Neil Armstrong to take his one small step, never dreaming what was to come.

BETTY LEHMAN LEWISBURG, KY

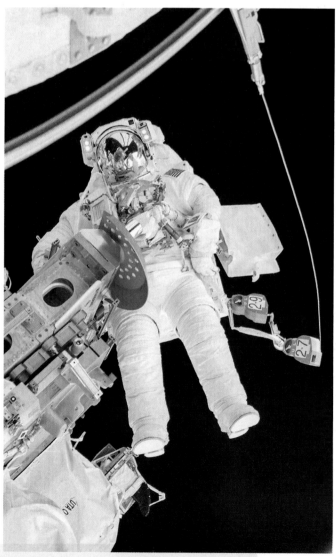

Betty's son-in-law Tim Kopra goes for a spacewalk. ★

SLIDESHOW OPENER IS JUST THE RIGHT STUFF

JOHN GLENN HELPS LAUNCH PROGRAM FOR HIGH SCHOOLERS.

As a relatively new professional with the Boy Scouts of America in 1969, I was intrigued by a program called Career Exploring. It gave boys and girls in high school hands-on experience with potential career opportunities.

My plan was to present the program at high school assemblies in my rural service area in New York. An opening slideshow would point out the different options in fields like law enforcement, medicine, law, firefighting, aviation and more. I wanted to add a recorded introduction from a well-known person. Anchorman Walter Cronkite declined, but Col. John Glenn agreed to do it. A date was set for me to meet him in New York City.

I packed a tape recorder, a camera and my script. My wife, Judy, came with me, and we went to the Royal Crown International offices on Madison Avenue, where Glenn was president. We met him in his office on the top floor, where he had us look out at a building under construction across the

street. He told us how long it took for each barrel of concrete to be taken up the side of the building to the 12th floor and be poured, an operation he'd timed. His engineering training was still apparent.

He made some changes to my script, and then he recorded his introduction. We chatted about the Career Exploring program, and he shared some stories about his Boy Scout days and earning the Eagle Scout award.

The slideshow was a big hit, and the Career Exploring program grew significantly. I was promoted to the BSA national office as national director of aviation exploring.

A photo of Glenn that I included in the slideshow still hangs in my office, as does one of him with Judy. I believe that the meeting with Col. Glenn, a kind and generous man, helped me as much as the students who joined the program.

FRANK LEWIS SAVANNAH, TX

Jazz musician and composer Duke Ellington poses for a studio portrait prior to his first European tour. ★

A GOLDEN AGE

MANY CREATIVE MINDS WERE BEHIND THE GREAT CULTURAL AWAKENING OF THE HARLEM RENAISSANCE.

The 1920s were in swing as writers, artists and musicians transformed the streets of New York City's Harlem neighborhood with a powerful mix of artistic, social and political work.

The cultural movement began with the Great Migration of African Americans from the rural South toward northern industrial hubs and their promise of jobs.

In urban centers, particularly Harlem, creativity challenged prejudice, shaped an identity and uplifted a new generation. Jazz was the sound of the Harlem Renaissance and Duke Ellington was a familiar figure at its center, but poets and painters—Langston Hughes, Jacob Lawrence—caught its rhythms, too.

The Harlem movement faded, like so much in the U.S., with the Great Depression, but it marked a turning point for Black culture. On the next few pages are some of the many artists who still inspire.

BY **NATALIE WYSONG**

DUKE ELLINGTON
1899-1974

THE JAZZ AGE PERMEATED literature, visual art, theater and dance, and no one better represented Harlem's golden era of creativity than composer and musician Edward "Duke" Ellington.

Ellington infused his music with his love of ragtime, and his diverse catalog of compositions—written to suit the styles of the performers at the Cotton Club—was challenging and complex. No two performances were alike.

Reaching audiences through live shows and radio broadcasts, Ellington elevated jazz, the American original, to an aesthetic.

LANGSTON HUGHES
1902-1967

IF THE LITERARY MOVEMENT HAD A CENTER, it was Langston Hughes, who recorded key first-person accounts about the era. His poetry drew from Black oral traditions and the rhythms of blues and jazz. In a poem he wrote just after graduating high school, *The Negro Speaks of Rivers*, Hughes traced African roots from the Mississippi River back to the Nile and the Euphrates.

Hughes was shaped by time spent abroad, and his insistence on expressing a strong sense of identity affected others in the movement, such as Lorraine Hansberry. Her Broadway play about the trauma of racism borrowed a line from Hughes' poem *Harlem*: "What happens to a dream deferred? Does it dry up like a raisin in the sun?"

ZORA NEALE HURSTON
1891-1960

BLACK-OWNED PUBLICATIONS IN NEW YORK catered to writers who were finally free to express themselves. They responded with a richness of poetry, essays and fiction about African American life.

Zora Neale Hurston was a native of the rural South, a folklorist and anthropologist. Her novel *Their Eyes Were Watching God* was about folk she knew. Overlooked for many years, Hurston's writing regained attention in the 1970s, thanks to Alice Walker.

Hurston followed in the footsteps of writers such as W.E.B. Du Bois and Jessie Redmon Fauset. Du Bois was a lifelong activist for equal treatment of Blacks, and founded the monthly magazine *The Crisis* in 1910. Fauset, the magazine's editor, identified promising writers and wrote novels dealing with race, class and identity.

PAUL ROBESON
1898-1976

WHEN *SHUFFLE ALONG* OPENED IN 1921, it upended ideas about Blacks on Broadway. In the chorus of the landmark musical was Paul Robeson, who started moonlighting on stage while practicing law. Robeson went on to groundbreaking achievement in roles that defied damaging minstrel-show stereotypes, playing characters in interracial romances in *Othello* and Eugene O'Neill's *All God's Chillun Got Wings*.

Showcasing African American talent, from writing to production, *Shuffle Along* and other musicals reached a wide audience and had lasting influence—the international craze for the Charleston dance was kicked off by *Runnin' Wild* (1924), for example.

AUGUSTA SAVAGE
1892-1962

SHOWN BELOW WITH HER SCULPTURE *Realization*, Augusta Savage was larger than life, a champion to Black artists who got a start in her Harlem studio.

Savage was drawn to sculpture as a child, using the distinctive red clay soil of her native Florida to mold figures. After studying abroad on fellowships, she ran a school out of her studio, offering free art education.

Much of her work did not survive. A commissioned piece for the 1939 New York World's Fair, a 16-foot sculpture with 12 singing figures, was destroyed after the fair. Savage worked mostly in plaster, rather than the conventional, and expensive, bronze. One existing sculpture in the Smithsonian's collection is *Gamin*, a bust of a young boy, which is done in plaster and painted to look like bronze.

LOUIS ARMSTRONG
1901-1971

JAZZ AROSE OUT OF THE BLACK AMERICAN EXPERIENCE, with a heritage of work songs, spirituals, blues, ragtime and African-style rhythms.

Louis Armstrong was part of the evolution of jazz from his youth in New Orleans to Joe "King" Oliver's Creole Jazz Band in Chicago. Bandleader Fletcher Henderson invited him to New York to play with his orchestra in 1924. In his acclaimed performances, Armstrong transferred the focus from the ensemble to the soloist.

Armstrong returned to Chicago after a year. He continued his rise, pushing the musical form in a way that influenced many other musicians and ushering jazz into the mainstream through recording with popular singers such as Bing Crosby.

For the next 50 years, Armstrong's playing shaped performers across the musical spectrum, an influence still felt today.

AARON DOUGLAS
1899-1979

THE ARCHITECT OF THE MOVEMENT to reconcile Black culture and history with contemporary American life was artist Aaron Douglas.

Douglas was a new high school art teacher in Kansas City, Missouri, when he felt drawn to the creative center of Harlem. He found work there—starting in the mailroom at *The Crisis*—and his collaborations with authors and essayists quickly gained attention for their dynamic African motifs.

His subjects were two-dimensional silhouettes of generic men and women, with a limited palette of circles and rays to show movement and draw focus. Some of Douglas' most famous works were the innovative and bold public murals that he painted for the Works Progress Administration's Federal Art Project.

Douglas went back to teaching, and later reflected that his proudest accomplishment was mentoring the next generation of artists.

BESSIE SMITH
1894-1937

BESSIE SMITH ON STAGE was powerful and majestic, and her recordings sold millions of copies. Orphaned, Smith was raised by her sister, and sang for money as a child. The Empress of the Blues sang about the kinds of trouble that most listeners knew well. Even when she was the highest paid Black performer of the day, her laments felt personal. She was criticized for being rough and bawdy, but songs like *'Taint*

Nobody's Biz-ness if I Do seemed to represent her feelings about others' opinions. In a world where the power was held by others, Smith defied prejudice and segregation to make listeners understand that her life mattered, too.

PACIFIST HERO

ONE MAN'S WAR STORY HAS A LASTING EFFECT.

When a conscientious objector became a Medal of Honor winner and World War I hero, it was a plot twist worthy of Hollywood.

Alvin Cullum York was a third-grade-educated Tennessee farmer and sharpshooter known for winning local turkey-shooting contests. A devout Christian from the backwater town of Pall Mall, he declared himself a pacifist when called to duty in WWI. His commanding officers convinced York that war, terrible as it is, can sometimes be justified. To help save the lives of those around him, he reluctantly agreed to become an infantryman.

In the waning days of the war, York killed 23 enemy combatants and managed to get 132 more to surrender. Allies France and Italy awarded him military honors, and he was given a hero's welcome when he returned stateside.

> ALLIES FRANCE AND ITALY AWARDED HIM MILITARY HONORS, AND HE WAS GIVEN A HERO'S WELCOME WHEN HE RETURNED STATESIDE.
>
> ★

Several Hollywood studios approached York about making a film, but he refused, not wanting his name to be used to glorify war.

By 1939, drums of war were again beating throughout Europe. In March 1940, York agreed to a filmed biography—but set some conditions, among them that a nonsmoking actress play his wife, Gracie, and that his own part be portrayed by superstar Gary Cooper.

For his part, Cooper was reluctant to play the role, though he later considered that bringing York's heroics to the screen was his contribution to the war effort.

An action-packed salute to wartime patriotism, Warner Bros.' *Sergeant York* became the biggest box-office hit of 1941 and brought Cooper his first of two Best Actor Oscars.

BY **RANDAL C. HILL**

Gary Cooper came to believe he had many things in common with the real-life hero he played in *Sergeant York*.

PATRIOTISM ON PARADE

MUSICAL PERFORMANCE GIVES FITTING TRIBUTE.

J ames Cagney was Hollywood's premier tough guy. He was best known as the star of a string of gangster films during the 1930s, including a genre-defining role as psychotic hoodlum Tom Powers in *The Public Enemy* (1931).

So in 1942, many moviegoers must have been surprised to see him singing and dancing in the musical *Yankee Doodle Dandy*, about veteran entertainer and songwriter George M. Cohan.

But as Cagney later explained, the role was not out of character for him. He'd cut his teeth as a musical performer in the 1920s. "I didn't have to pretend to be a song-and-dance man," he said. "I was one."

At 43, the 5-foot-4-inch Cagney brought his legendary charisma to this iconic biopic. It opens with Cohan being summoned to the White House, thus setting the scene for Cohan to reflect on his

life and that of his vaudeville family through a series of flashbacks.

A thick slice of apple-pie patriotism, *Yankee Doodle Dandy* paid monumental tribute to Cohan, long the grand gentleman of musical theater and king of Broadway. It also served as a fitting coda, coming out only a few months before Cohan died.

Many of Cohan's most-loved songs are here: "The Yankee Doodle Boy," "You're a Grand Old Flag," "Over There" and "Give My Regards to Broadway."

Both Cagney and Cohan were proud of the unabashed flag-waving in the movie, an antidote to the pall of war that clouded American life in the early 1940s.

The role was a highlight of Cagney's impressive six-decade career. As Cohan himself said of the performance: "My God, what an act to follow!"

> A THICK SLICE OF APPLE-PIE PATRIOTISM, *YANKEE DOODLE DANDY* PAID MONUMENTAL TRIBUTE TO COHAN.

BY **RANDAL C. HILL**

Rod Serling once said, "My diet consisted chiefly of black coffee and fingernails."

BEHIND THAT VOICE

THERE'S MORE THAN MEETS THE EYE TO THIS SCI-FI LEGEND.

R od Serling started writing TV scripts in his 20s, winning Emmys in 1956, '57 and '58, but often battled program censors and sponsors who found his work too controversial. In 1959, Serling cannily turned to science fiction. In the creepy "fifth dimension" of *The Twilight Zone*, which debuted that October, social commentary breezed past censors while still delivering an emotional wallop. Serling would win three more Emmys, two for *Twilight Zone* scripts, and was inducted into the Television Academy Hall of Fame in 1985.

Serling earned a Purple Heart and a Bronze Star in WWII. He was injured while serving with the Army in the Philippines. Flashbacks and nightmares haunted him for years afterward.

His now famous narration was actually Plan B. Serling framed each episode of *The Twilight Zone* with a riveting, clipped delivery, but had wanted actor Richard Egan—and no one else—to do it.

> ## FLASHBACKS AND NIGHTMARES HAUNTED HIM FOR YEARS AFTERWARD.

When that didn't work out, Serling said he'd do it himself.

That voice was as distinctive as Serling's writing. From 1968 to 1974, he narrated 28 episodes of *The Undersea World of Jacques Cousteau*.

Serling was his own toughest critic. In his last interview, on March 4, 1975, he was loath to call anything he'd written "important," and thought that only his teleplays "Requiem for a Heavyweight" ('56), and "They're Tearing Down Tim Riley's Bar," from *Night Gallery* ('69-'73), would stand the test of time.

In 2004, *TV Guide* rated him No. 1 on its list of 25 Greatest Sci-Fi Legends. Everyone else was a fictional character. *Star Trek* crews came in at No. 2, but the series creator, Serling's friend Gene Roddenberry, didn't make the list. Roddenberry gave the eulogy at Serling's funeral.

BY **DEB WARLAUMONT MULVEY**

CELEBRITY SELLS

The timeless appeal of a star never disappoints.

Enter to Win

What would this ad for Noxzema be without Perry Como's face on it (twice) and his special jingle for the contest? And the prizes sure are attractive, especially the portable TV set with a handle on top. It's fun to think of the places you could take it.

FRANKIE WOWS THE PARAMOUNT

HE SET THE STAGE FOR SCREAMFESTS TO COME.

Benny Goodman was to close 1942 as the headliner at the prestigious Paramount Theatre in New York City. At the last minute, Paramount manager Bob Weitman signed a young, little-known male vocalist as an added attraction.

Weitman was intrigued that, one week before at a New Jersey venue, the scrawny 27-year-old with a floppy bow tie had caused young women to screech their throats raw when he crooned.

Frank Sinatra, pursuing a solo career after leaving the Tommy Dorsey Orchestra three months earlier, closed Goodman's show on Dec. 30, 1942. After Goodman's straightforward introduction— "And now, Frank Sinatra"—a tidal wave of screams from the packed house caught the bandleader off guard. Sinatra offered up "For Me and My Gal."

> ## THE SCRAWNY 27-YEAR-OLD WITH A FLOPPY BOW TIE HAD CAUSED YOUNG WOMEN TO SCREECH.
> ★

Veteran press agent George Evans was hired to spread the word about the rising star. The crafty Evans auditioned young women to select those with the loudest shrieks and placed them strategically throughout the audience, coaching them to scream when Sinatra launched into a dreamy ballad. They were paid $5—a tidy sum at a time when the federal minimum wage was 30 cents an hour.

The ploy proved to be unnecessary: Hundreds of his fans, who became known as bobby-soxers, screamed and swooned for free.

Sinatra's engagement at the Paramount was extended, and in 1943, The Voice became a superstar.

BY **RANDAL C. HILL**

Sinatra stands on a stepladder to sign autographs amid a sea of fans in Los Angeles in 1943.

EIGHT TO THE BAR

ANDREWS SISTERS TUNE CARRIED THE COUNTRY THROUGH THE WAR.

When Bette Midler's rendition of "Boogie Woogie Bugle Boy" became an Atlantic Records Top 10 single in 1973, a new generation of music fans embraced an iconic tune whose origins had faded.

The popular Andrews Sisters—LaVerne, Maxene and Patty—had harmonized the song in the 1941 Abbott and Costello film *Buck Privates*. The bouncy ditty became a patriotic Decca Records smash for the beloved sibling warblers.

Written by Don Raye and Hughie Prince, it seems connected to World War II, but it was recorded in January 1941, 11 months before the Pearl Harbor attack, and shortly after the FDR administration imposed the first peacetime military draft.

The frantic-paced "Boogie Woogie Bugle Boy" featured a storyline—fun but hardly realistic—about a hip Chicago street musician/draftee. Without his bandmates, he can't do justice to blowing an upbeat reveille call when he's ordered to play it to begin each morning. His company commander ("the Cap") saves the day by assembling a barracks band to offer a spirited wake-up call for the snoozing soldiers.

Music historians sometimes erroneously credit the story's inspiration to Chicago-based musician Clarence Zylman (who actually hailed from Muskegon, Michigan) as the real-life "boogie woogie bugle boy." But Zylman enlisted in the Army—he wasn't drafted—on June 9, 1942, long after the song became a hit.

BY **RANDAL C. HILL**

Charles and his backing vocalists, the Raelettes.

RAY CHARLES STRIKES GOLD

RIFFING, HE MADE IT LOOK EASY.

Playing a dance hall in Pittsburgh, Pennsylvania, in December 1958, Ray Charles and his seven-piece band ran through their entire repertoire and then realized they had some time to fill.

Knowing the band had to finish the four-hour set to get paid, Charles dug deep and came up with a groovable beat and simple lyrics—mostly oohs and aahs—that lit up the crowd.

"There was nothing left that I could think of," Charles recalled in *Brother Ray: Ray Charles' Own Story*.

"So I finally said to the band and the Raelettes, 'Listen, I'm going to fool around and y'all just follow me.'"

A blues-based boogie-woogie riff on his electric keyboard set the stage. Then Charles began tossing out short lyric lines, which he encouraged the backup singers to repeat in a church-style call and response.

The dance crowd went wild, and Ray later remembered, "When I got through, folks came up and asked me where they could buy the record. 'Ain't no record,' I said, 'just something I made up to kill a little time.'"

Recorded a few months later in New York City, the song was released in June 1959. "What'd I Say" blended rhythm and blues, gospel and jazz in the relatively new style of soul.

That summer, Charles' disc reached No. 1 on the R&B charts and crossed over to No. 6 on the pop lists, bringing him a new audience—white teens who were enthralled by a sound that was boldly different, irresistibly sexy and extremely danceable.

Charles already had a number of hit singles, but the serendipitous song he created to run out the clock became his first official gold record, and today it is regarded as one of the best of the early rock era.

BY **RANDAL C. HILL**

NATURAL TALENT

THE LEGACY OF MILES DAVIS WILL NOT BE FORGOTTEN.

By his own account, trumpeter Miles Davis "changed music five or six times." *Birth of the Cool*, released in 1957 but recorded when Davis was in his early 20s, marked one such shift. The album's innovative sound, which included French horn and tuba, was the blueprint for a new jazz genre, and the musicians Davis assembled for three separate recording sessions in 1949 and '50 showed his genius for collaboration. One critic complained that the album was "not really jazz," but today, it's regarded as nothing short of revolutionary.

Miles Dewey Davis III was raised in East St. Louis, Illinois. His dentist father started him on private trumpet lessons at 13. In 1944, Davis performed with jazz greats Charlie Parker and Dizzy Gillespie.

Davis enrolled in Juilliard in 1944, adding extracurricular jazz sessions in New York's clubs at night. He left Juilliard in 1945, once again joining Parker to record his first original compositions.

DAVIS PLAYED THE TRUMPET WITH ALMOST NO VIBRATO.

★

Tone became his trademark. Davis played the trumpet with almost no vibrato, creating a lyrical voice distinct from other jazz musicians—think Louis Armstrong's technical mastery of high notes. Davis' use of a mute to diffuse the sound lent an otherworldly quality to his music.

He pushed boundaries. After *Birth of the Cool*, Davis turned to other jazz styles, and in 1955 formed a quintet whose cutting-edge performances reached a peak with 1959's *Kind of Blue*, the top-selling jazz album of all time. Known as the Dark Prince, on stage he came across as solemn and brooding, which wasn't helped by his habit of turning his back on audiences. He disliked smiling for photos, believing it bolstered an image of deferential Black entertainers.

He won eight Grammys. Nominated 32 times, Davis won his first Grammy in 1960 and received a Lifetime Achievement Award in 1990.

BY **NATALIE WYSONG**

Miles Davis would say, "Don't play what's there, play what's not there."

TWO BUDDIES KIDDING AROUND

THE DAY THE MUSIC DIED WAS A SAD DAY FOR ALL.

Roger Peterson was excited. The 21-year-old Iowa pilot was about to fly three of the biggest rock stars—Charles Hardin "Buddy" Holly, 22; Ritchie Valens, 17; and The Big Bopper (J.P. Richardson), 28—to Fargo, North Dakota, their next stop. Each had paid $36—about $300 today—for a place on the four-seater plane. Holly's backup band, initially scheduled to fly with him, consisted of two then-unknown musicians, guitarist Tommy Allsup and bassist Waylon Jennings.

Chartering the 1947 Beechcraft Bonanza was Holly's idea. The grinding Midwest tour (dubbed the Winter Dance Party) had proven wretched. Their school bus often broke down in whiteout conditions. Enough was enough.

On the night of Feb. 2, 1959, the musicians, along with supporting act Dion and the Belmonts,

> **THEIR SCHOOL BUS OFTEN BROKE DOWN IN WHITEOUT CONDITIONS.**

rocked the Surf Ballroom in Clear Lake, Iowa, for 1,500 fans—with Holly as the Belmonts' surprise drummer.

Hours later, at the nearby Mason City airport, The Big Bopper, sick with the flu, took Jennings' place. Valens won guitarist Allsup's seat after a last-minute coin toss.

A light snow was falling when the plane took off just before 1 a.m., only to go down—no one knows why—in a pitch-dark cornfield five minutes later. All aboard perished.

Just before heading to the airport, Holly called out to his bandmate Jennings, "I hope your ol' bus freezes up again!" Jennings countered with the retort: "Well, I hope your ol' plane crashes!"

BY **RANDAL C. HILL**

Ritchie Valens takes the mike. Don McLean's 1971 hit "American Pie" memorialized rock's first tragedy.

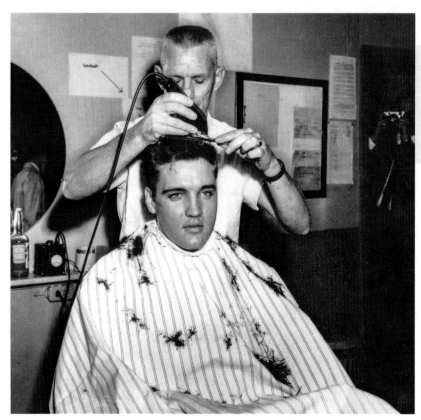

U.S. ARMY PRIVATE #53310761

ELVIS PRESLEY HAD SOMETHING TO PROVE.

March 24, 1958—called Black Monday by the media—was a tragic day for rock 'n' roll fans: At the zenith of his career, 23-year-old Army draftee Elvis Aron Presley became an ordinary buck private beginning a two-year commitment to his country's defense.

Elvis was finishing *King Creole*, his fourth movie, in 1957 when his manager, Colonel Tom Parker, procured a deferment for Presley from the Memphis Draft Board until filming was completed.

Presley could have agreed to the military's cushy options— playing for the troops or serving as a recruiting model—but he declined special treatment. His induction won over former critics—parents, teachers, religious leaders— who had viewed him as a nuisance or even a threat.

He showed no sign of regret on the day that broke millions of teenage hearts. He underwent a physical, took aptitude tests and endured a GI haircut. Assigned as the leader of his group, Presley and a dozen others were bused from Memphis to Fort Chaffee, Arkansas, and soon afterward to Fort Hood, Texas, for basic training. Later, he shipped out for Germany.

"People were expecting me to mess up, to goof up in one way or another," he said later. "They thought I couldn't take it and so forth, and I was determined to go to any limits to prove otherwise— not only to the people who were wondering, but to myself."

> PRESLEY COULD HAVE AGREED TO THE MILITARY'S CUSHY OPTIONS—PLAYING FOR THE TROOPS OR SERVING AS A RECRUITING MODEL.
>
> ★

BY **RANDAL C. HILL**

★ ★ ★ **FACE TO FACE** ★ ★ ★

Head over heels for pop stars of the '50s and '60s, my older sister
Anne-Marie met the singing sensation from South Philly, Frankie Avalon,
more than once and got his autograph to boot.

MONICA ROSE GABOR RIVERDALE, MD